180 PRAYERS
FOR A HOPEFUL HEART

Lord, I Need You

JANICE
THOMPSON

BARBOUR
PUBLISHING

*To my grandson, Isaac Ames Morrow.
God knew before you were born who and what
you would be. We can't wait to see His plans
fulfilled in your life, little man! Nina loves you.*

SECTION ONE: "FOR I KNOW"

"For I know the plans I have for you," declares the Lord, "plans to prosper you and not to harm you, plans to give you hope and a future."

JEREMIAH 29:11 NIV

Isn't it comforting to realize that God knows all of the details of our lives—our yesterdays, our todays, our tomorrows—even when we don't? Think about that for a moment. God knew you before you were born. He understands the pains you've suffered in the past. God hears the questions going through your mind today. He knows what's coming around the bend. Most of all, God knows your heart. He's aware of your ambitions, your tolerance level, your limitations. He's also keenly aware of your breaking point. He understands and appreciates your desires and even rushes to your rescue when you need His intervention. God knows who to surround you with. He knows how to pick you up when you fall. God knows how to awaken dreams in you once again. And because the King of creation knows all of these things, we don't have to. We can trust Him in the *not* knowing. Not knowing makes for an adventure, wouldn't you agree? When you can't see around the bend, when the twists and turns leave you discombobulated, God is right there, leading and guiding, full of knowledge and wisdom. We can take comfort in the fact that our all-knowing God has amazing plans for us, plans to bring us good and not evil.

All-Knowing

*Oh, the depth of the riches both of the wisdom
and knowledge of God! How unsearchable
are His judgments and His ways past finding
out! "For who has known the mind of the
Lord? Or who has become His counselor?"*

ROMANS 11:33–34 NKJV

You know, Lord! Even when I don't, You know all things about my journey—which road I should take, which decisions I should make, which plans are established for me. You also know how to speak to my heart and offer guidance every step of the way. You are my all-knowing Father, the only One who truly has my best interest at heart. I settle the issue once and for all, this very day. I trust You to lead me according to Your sovereign will. Amen.

Like-Minded with My Father

Then God said, "Let us make human beings in our image, to be like us. They will reign over the fish in the sea, the birds in the sky, the livestock, all the wild animals on the earth, and the small animals that scurry along the ground."

GENESIS 1:26 NLT

I don't always know or understand Your thoughts, Lord; but I am created in Your image, which gives me glimpses into Your will for my life. Thank You for giving me the mind of Christ. What a privilege, to be like-minded with You, Lord! May my heart beat in sync with Yours and may my thought life respond as You guide my every step. Amen.

His Ways Are Higher

"For my thoughts are not your thoughts, neither are your ways my ways," declares the LORD.

ISAIAH 55:8 NIV

Your ways are higher, Lord. It's not always clear in the moment, but my plans—great as they might seem—don't even come close to Yours, simply because You see what I can't see. You know what I don't know. You care in ways I simply cannot comprehend. When the road You're leading me down makes no sense to my finite mind, Father, sweep in and remind me that Your thoughts, Your ways are always higher. Amen.

A Glimpse Inside

*"Call to me and I will answer you and tell you
great and unsearchable things you do not know."*

JEREMIAH 33:3 NIV

I'm so grateful for the times when You pull back the curtain, Lord, and give me tiny glimpses into Your plans for my life. I can hardly comprehend the magnificence of Your thought process, but Your love is overwhelming during these "glimpsing" seasons. What a privilege to walk through life with Your hand so tightly clasped in my own. What a joy to know that I can trust You implicitly. And how generous and kind You are, Lord. All You ask is that I call on You, so today I choose to do that with my whole heart. Amen.

You Look at My Heart

But the LORD said to Samuel, "Do not consider his appearance or his height, for I have rejected him. The LORD does not look at the things people look at. People look at the outward appearance, but the LORD looks at the heart."

1 SAMUEL 16:7 NIV

Lord, it troubles me to see how much interest people put in outward appearance. Clothing. Shoes. Makeup. Hairstyles. These things are fine, but when they become the focus—the primary things people notice—something is amiss. I'm so glad You're not examining me from the outside in, making sure I measure up to society's standards. Thank You for looking at my heart. Not that my heart is perfect, as You well know, but You're so good at ironing out the wrinkles when things are off-kilter internally. What a gracious God You are. Amen.

We Know in Part

For now we see only a reflection as in a mirror;
then we shall see face to face. Now I know in part;
then I shall know fully, even as I am fully known.

1 CORINTHIANS 13:12 NIV

I'll admit it, Lord—there have been times in my life when I've acted like a know-it-all. I've tried to show up others or prove they were wrong and I was right. I must confess that I don't know it all, Father. Only You can claim that. I know in part. You know in full. It boggles my mind to think about the scope of Your knowledge, especially when it comes to the plans You've made for my life. I trust not in what I do or don't know, but in You, the All-Knowing. You've got me covered, Father. Bless You for that! Amen.

Perfectly Knitted

You have searched me, LORD, and you know me.
You know when I sit and when I rise; you
perceive my thoughts from afar. You discern my
going out and my lying down; you are familiar
with all my ways. . . . Such knowledge is too
wonderful for me, too lofty for me to attain.

PSALM 139:1–3, 6 NIV

When I ponder the fact that Your work in my life began even before You knit me together in my mother's womb, I'm floored, Father. You thought this out, long before I came into being. You went to so much trouble just to make me who I am. You know everything about, well, *everything*—and that brings such comfort. I know I can trust You, my Creator, to guide me every step of the way. Amen.

You Know the Heart

"Forgive and act; deal with everyone according
to all they do, since you know their hearts
(for you alone know every human heart),
so that they will fear you all the time they
live in the land you gave our ancestors."

1 KINGS 8:39–40 NIV

Only You know the motivations of others, Lord.
I question people all the time—wondering where
their hearts are, wondering why they do the
things they do. Why they choose to hurt others.
Why they fall down on the job. Why they don't
follow through. Why they break promises. It's not
mine to question, Father, but to trust that You will
speak to the deepest places in their hearts. I can
trust You to know what's going on, deep inside
each of us. I praise You for that! Amen.

You Made the Day

This is the day the LORD has made.
We will rejoice and be glad in it.

PSALM 118:24 NLT

When I ponder the fact that time is in Your hands and that You created days, hours, minutes, and seconds, I realize that each and every nano-second is Yours to do with as You please. If You created these things, they are Yours to manage. I don't have to fret over the items on my to-do list that don't get done today, Father. All I ask is that You—my perfect, all-knowing Father—guide my steps. I will do my best to rejoice in this day, Lord, and to be happy knowing You are in control and I'm not. (Whew, what a relief!) Amen.

Full to the Brim

For the earth shall be full of the knowledge
of the LORD, as the waters cover the sea.

ISAIAH 11:9 KJV

Father, what an amazing picture You have painted
with this verse. Your knowledge is too lofty for me.
I cannot attain it. But I can picture it spread out like
mighty rushing waters across this planet, covering
vast areas. My thoughts hardly compare to Yours.
They are minute in comparison. But You invite me
to share glimpses, to see that Your ways—though
higher—are better for me than my own. How could
I not trust a God who sees all, knows all, and guides
all? I trust You, Lord. Amen.

All-Seeing

The eyes of the LORD are everywhere,
keeping watch on the wicked and the good.

PROVERBS 15:3 NIV

My vision is so limited, Father. I can only see what's right in front of me. (And sometimes—especially when I'm looking for something specific, like my keys or phone—I can't even see what's right in front of me.) I certainly can't see what's happening one street over or in another city. Yet You see all. You are witness to every action, every word, every thought. Because You see, I can trust You, Lord. Oh, how blessed I am that my heavenly Father has twenty-twenty vision! Amen.

Yet to Be Revealed

Dear friends, now we are children of God, and
what we will be has not yet been made known.
But we know that when Christ appears, we
shall be like him, for we shall see him as he is.
1 JOHN 3:2 NIV

My vision is so cloudy at times, Lord. I can't see what's coming around the next bend, let alone where You're taking me in this coming season of my life. (Oh, how I wish I could!) Trusting You when I can't see is a bit like walking on water. I don't always have the security of knowing that my eyes won't deceive me, and sometimes I feel like I'm going under. But I know I can trust You, Father. You haven't let me drown yet. I'll keep my eyes on You, Lord. Amen.

With All My Heart

"Then you will call on me and come and pray to me, and I will listen to you. You will seek me and find me when you seek me with all your heart."

JEREMIAH 29:12–13 NIV

Here's a little confession, Lord: I often do things halfheartedly. Housework. Laundry. Tasks at my job. This is difficult to admit, but I don't always give my relationship with You 100 percent, either. Of course, You already know that. You see my motivation (or lack thereof). I'm so sorry, Father. It feels good to make that confession because I want to be an "all-in" sort of girl, one who seeks You with my whole heart. Give me the push I need, even when I don't feel like it, Lord. Amen.

Perfect Vision

But, as it is written, "What no eye has seen, nor ear heard, nor the heart of man imagined, what God has prepared for those who love him"—these things God has revealed to us through the Spirit. For the Spirit searches everything, even the depths of God.

1 CORINTHIANS 2:9—10 ESV

My vision isn't always the best, Lord. I can see only with my physical eyes most of the time. There's so much more to see when the veil is pulled back. What's going on up there in the heavenly realms? I can only imagine all of the amazing things You're planning, even now. I get so excited when I think about Your goodness, Your heart for me. Even now, Your Spirit is searching deep places, putting the pieces of the puzzle in place. Oh, to have Your heavenly vision, Lord! Can I have a little glimpse? Please? Amen.

Made from the Invisible

By faith we understand that the universe was formed at God's command, so that what is seen was not made out of what was visible.

HEBREWS 11:3 NIV

Life is like a giant puzzle to me at times, Lord, only the puzzle pieces aren't always clear. Sometimes I feel like I'm groping around in the dark, trying to force things together. I can't always get the pieces to fit. Oh, but You have the perfect plan all prepared in advance. There's no need to force anything, is there? What I can't see, You can. When I can't fit the invisible pieces together, You shuffle the board in Your own creative way and make things crystal clear so that I only move when I feel led by Your Spirit. Trusting when my vision isn't clear isn't always easy, but You make it worth it, Father. Thank You! Amen.

Measuring Stick

Great is our Lord, and abundant in power;
his understanding is beyond measure.

PSALM 147:5 ESV

It's remarkable to think about Your level of understanding, Father. It's beyond measure. You "get" it—all the time. There's never a situation You don't understand. There's never a problem You can't solve. There's never a relationship issue You can't navigate. There's never a question You can't answer. Oh, how I wish I had Your measuring stick, Lord. For now, though, I'll lean on the fact that Your ability to move on my behalf is all I need. I'm so grateful for that, Lord! Amen.

A Light on My Path

Your word is a lamp for my feet,
a light on my path.

PSALM 119:105 NIV

I know what it's like to stumble around in the dark, Lord. Toes get stubbed. Knees get bumped. Things get knocked over. Sure, my eyes adjust to a certain extent, but I'm still second-guessing myself because things aren't as clear as they should be. I can't make out the road signs. But You provide a light, Father. When I'm feeling unsure, I ask You to brighten my path so that I don't cause damage as I move along. I'm glad You illuminate the road for me, Lord. I praise You for that. Amen.

Your Counsel Stands

Declaring the end from the beginning, and from ancient times the things that are not yet done, saying, My counsel shall stand, and I will do all my pleasure.

ISAIAH 46:10 KJV

Because You see all and know all, You can be trusted with not just my life but my family, my community, my state, my country—the whole of humankind, in fact. When the news on TV is bad, I can trust You, Father. When things are falling apart politically, You're still on the throne. You know best how to reach the hearts of those who need change, Father. Help me release any anxieties and rest in the knowledge that You know and You care. Your counsel stands, Lord. How mighty You are! Amen.

No Hiding

Neither is there any creature that is not manifest in his sight: but all things are naked and opened unto the eyes of him with whom we have to do.

HEBREWS 4:13 KJV

All things are visible to You, Father. Your kids don't get away with shenanigans because You're an all-seeing God. We are like babes on the changing table, naked and bare before You. There's not a thing about us You don't know: our angst, bitterness, concerns, joys. But You don't leave us to wallow in our woes, Father. (Thank goodness!) Just as a mother changes her child, You are ready to step in and change our hearts. Praise You for seeking us out, Lord. Amen.

Revealed through the Spirit

These are the things God has revealed to us
by his Spirit. The Spirit searches all things,
even the deep things of God. For who knows
a person's thoughts except their own spirit
within them? In the same way no one knows
the thoughts of God except the Spirit of God.

1 CORINTHIANS 2:10–11 NIV

Sometimes I forget, Lord. I forget that revelation only comes through You. I want to obtain answers—direction—in the usual ways: from friends, loved ones, acquaintances. Even from my own knowledge, obtained from years of walking this planet. Advice is good. Knowledge is good. But I need to hear Your thoughts. Learning to quiet myself and listen to that still, small voice isn't my first inclination, Father. Thank You for the reminder that You've got answers to whisper in my ear, things yet to be revealed. Amen.

SECTION TWO: HIS PLANS

"For I know the plans I have for you," declares
the LORD, *"plans to prosper you and not to harm
you, plans to give you hope and a future."*

JEREMIAH 29:11 NIV

How often we forget that God's plans are far superior to our own. We set our sights on a goal and aim hard, determined to move forward. Then we wonder why things don't work out. Oh, but God doesn't work that way. He longs to surprise us with new ideas, new dreams, new visions. What a creative God we serve. He breathes life into motion. And our heavenly Father maps out every detail. Nothing is left to chance. Perhaps the most exciting news is that the word *plans* in Jeremiah 29:11 is plural. When we get off course and things go awry, our creative God is capable of sending us down a new road. Isn't it wonderful to realize His plans are specific to you, taking into account your personality, your gifts, and your joys? No one can advise you on His plans as well as He can. And while His plans might not always make sense in the moment, we trust in the fact that God is an amazing architect. What He's building in us is for our benefit. Let's praise Him for His creative plans!

He Guides Me Along

He lets me rest in green pastures. He leads me to calm water. He gives me new strength. He leads me on paths that are right for the good of his name.

PSALM 23:2—3 NCV

Father, what a good trailblazer You are! You guide me along all of the right paths, the ones You've chosen just for me. I acknowledge that Your plans are better than my own. I can set my foot on a path, but if it's not the one You designed for me, then it will get me nowhere. So, I don't just trust in Your guidance, Father, but in the plan too. I can imagine You've got great heavenly blueprints with my name all over them. I submit to the building process, Lord. Amen.

Do Not Fear

"So do not fear, for I am with you; do not be dismayed,
for I am your God. I will strengthen you and help you;
I will uphold you with my righteous right hand."

ISAIAH 41:10 NIV

Maybe it's just my controlling nature, Father, but I have a hard time not being afraid. You ask me to take my hands off, to let You be in charge. The idea of letting go of the reins is frightening. But today I choose to let go of fear as I release my hold on the reins of my life. (They were never mine to hold in the first place, were they?) And while trusting Your plans for my life is hard, I know You will grow my faith with each step I take. I also know You're working for my good, Lord. Thank You for that. Amen.

Engraved on Your Palms

"See, I have engraved you on the palms of my hands; your walls are ever before me."

ISAIAH 49:16 NIV

Lord, You care so deeply for me. I am in wonder and awe as I think about the fact that Your plans for my life are engraved on Your hands. Oh, those wonderful, perfect hands! They lead me, they guide me, they lift me up when I fall. And what an amazing thought, to know that You care enough about me to carry a permanent marking of love. How can I praise You for caring so deeply for me, Father? I stand amazed. Amen.

Not in Himself

*LORD, I know that people's lives are not their
own; it is not for them to direct their steps.*

JEREMIAH 10:23 NIV

The world tells me to look within, Lord. I'm told
that everything I need to know about myself, for
myself, is already inside me. Oh, Father, what a
foolish notion! The answers aren't found in me.
I can plan and devise all I like, but the only true
answers are found in You. If I set my own course,
I'm sure to land in a ditch. You direct my path. You
make the plans. I'll do my best to lean close and
listen as You lead me along a better path. Amen.

He Will Fulfill

The LORD will fulfill his purpose for me;
your steadfast love, O LORD, endures forever.
Do not forsake the work of your hands.

PSALM 138:8 ESV

So many projects around my house are unfinished, Lord. My intentions are good, but my desire to carry through often wanes. Not so with You. You always fulfill Your purposes. If You start something in my life, I can trust You to complete it. May I learn from Your example, Father. I don't just want to be someone who "gets off to a great start." Lord, I long to be a person who finishes well. Help me as I strive to become more like You, Father. Amen.

His Workmanship

*For we are his workmanship, created in Christ
Jesus for good works, which God prepared
beforehand, that we should walk in them.*

EPHESIANS 2:10 ESV

Oh, how I love this verse, Father! I picture You as
a wood-carver, Lord, shaping me into a thing of
beauty. Your Son, Jesus, is the model, and You are
carving His image as my life moves along. I would
imagine there are some seasons where I stubbornly
refuse to be molded. Forgive me for those times,
Lord. I want to be pliable in Your hands, someone
You can be proud of. What an honor to be Your
workmanship, Lord. You are the Master Artist,
after all, and I submit myself to the process, Your
willing child. Amen.

His Purposes

*"I know that you can do all things, and that
no purpose of yours can be thwarted."*

JOB 42:2 ESV

God, it's remarkable to think about the fact that
You are capable of doing all things. There's not a
thing You've ever tried that You didn't accomplish.
Me? I try and fail all the time. I can't even imagine
what it must feel like to have a 100 percent success
rate. (How amazing would that be?) Because You're
the ultimate example of success, I know I can trust
You to successfully plan my future. You won't make
any mistakes. Me? If You'd put me in charge, I'm
pretty sure I would've messed things up in a big
way. Today I'm so grateful that no purpose of
Yours can be thwarted. Amen.

Superglue

And he is before all things, and in
him all things hold together.

COLOSSIANS 1:17 ESV

Father, You're like cosmic superglue. You hold all things together. When I make plans, they often crumble. I set off on the right path, and before long, things come unraveled. With You behind the wheel, things stick together. The plan works out. No unraveling. No crumbling. That's because You've got the power to hold things steady, even when everything around me is shaking. Have I mentioned how grateful I am for that? Praise You, Lord! I'll stick with You as You stick with the plan. Amen.

That All Might Be Saved

This is good, and pleases God our Savior,
who wants all people to be saved and to
come to a knowledge of the truth.

1 TIMOTHY 2:3–4 NIV

Of all the plans You've set in motion, Lord, this one's my favorite. It is Your good and perfect will that all will be saved. All—everyone! People across this beautiful planet are all loved by You (even people who are radically different from me). Thank You for including me in the plan to reach people with the Gospel, Father. May I be an example to all of Your love, Your grace, Your peace. And while I'm waiting for those around me to come to a knowledge of the truth, may I exemplify Your gracious heart toward them. Amen.

Perseverance

You need to persevere so that when you
have done the will of God, you will
receive what he has promised.

HEBREWS 10:36 NIV

Lord, I so often reach the point of giving up when I'm following my own path. Somehow, knowing You're the One with the plan gives me the wherewithal to keep going. I'll persevere, Father, because I know You're ultimately the One in charge. I submit myself to Your will and Your process, Lord. It's not always easy, but I will do my best to put one foot in front of the other as I walk out this remarkable plan You've set in motion for my life. Amen.

Fixed by His Authority

*He said to them: "It is not for you to
know the times or dates the Father
has set by his own authority."*

ACTS 1:7 NIV

We are ruled by the clock, Lord. It tells us when to wake up, when to go to work, when to eat, when to sleep. The hours and minutes are fixed. Set. Always the same, day after day. Your times are fixed too, Lord. When You set a plan in motion, it has a timeline. And though I can't see this timeline, I can trust in the fact that it was set in place by Your authority. I can trust Your timetable, Father. I choose to trust, even when it appears to throw me off course. Amen.

Acquainted with All My Ways

You know when I sit and when I rise; you perceive my thoughts from afar. You discern my going out and my lying down; you are familiar with all my ways.

PSALM 139:2—3 NIV

I often use the phrase "No one knows me like I know myself," but that's not true, Lord. You know me better than I know myself. You know every detail—my likes, my dislikes, my hopes, my dreams, my disappointments, my joys. You're acquainted not only with the things I've done in the past but also with what I hope to accomplish in the future. Because You know me from the inside out, I am confident in Your ability to scrutinize my path and make a way for me. It's exciting to see where You will take me next, Lord. Amen.

The Teacher of All Things

"But the Advocate, the Holy Spirit, whom the Father will send in my name, will teach you all things and will remind you of everything I have said to you."
JOHN 14:26 NIV

My ability to retain the things I learned in school is limited at best. And, while I'd like to consider myself to be a good student, Lord, I often fall short—even when You're trying to teach me a life lesson. Thank You for sending Your Helper, the Holy Spirit. What a blessing, to know that Your plans for my life will all become clearer with His help. You are the Teacher of all things, Father, which means that You have high hopes for me! I'm so grateful, Lord. Amen.

That Your Joy May Be Full

"I have told you this so that my joy may be in you and that your joy may be complete."

JOHN 15:11 NIV

It gives me great joy to plan things, Lord. Christmas dinner, parties, family gatherings—I love putting those plans together. And I do it all with others in mind. I can envision the looks on their faces as they partake of the foods I've made, the packages I've wrapped. What joy it must bring You to create plans for my life. Thank You for allowing that joy to spill over as I walk out the path You have laid for me. You've done it all with me in mind, and I'm forever grateful. Praise You, Father! Amen.

A Way of Escape

*The Lord knoweth how to deliver the godly
out of temptations, and to reserve the unjust
unto the day of judgment to be punished.*

2 PETER 2:9 KJV

I feel like I'm trapped in a dark alley at times, Lord, with no escape route. My own actions—well intentioned as they might be at times—take me to places that leave me feeling stuck. Oh, but how wonderful Your plans are! You always provide a way of escape for me, even when I've painted myself into a corner. Thank You for coming to my rescue, Father. I can't promise it won't happen again, but I do promise to resist temptation with Your help. Amen.

Strengthened with Power

*For this reason I kneel before the Father,
from whom every family in heaven and on
earth derives its name. I pray that out of his
glorious riches he may strengthen you with
power through his Spirit in your inner being.*

EPHESIANS 3:14–16 NIV

It's a glorious feeling, Father, to wake up feeling so refreshed, so energized, that I could take the world by storm. That's what it's like after spending time in Your presence too. When I take the time to bring my needs and my concerns to You, I leave feeling much better. You pour out Your Spirit, and that amazing supernatural energy of Yours empowers me. I can't drum up this kind of power, Father. It comes only from You. I'm so very grateful for Your strength, Lord! Amen.

For My Sake

Jesus said, "I tell you the truth, all those who have left houses, brothers, sisters, mother, father, children, or farms for me and for the Good News will get more than they left. Here in this world they will have a hundred times more homes, brothers, sisters, mothers, children, and fields. And with those things, they will also suffer for their belief. But in this age they will have life forever."

MARK 10:29–30 NCV

I hear it all the time, Lord. People say things like "I'd do anything for my family" or "Don't mess with my kids or grandkids!" Folks are protective of their own. Lord, today I ask You to give me that kind of passion for my relationship with You. May I be so protective of my time with You, so grateful for Your plans for my life that I fight to keep You in Your rightful place. Amen.

To Prepare a Place

*"My Father's house has many rooms; if that were
not so, would I have told you that I am going there
to prepare a place for you? And if I go and prepare
a place for you, I will come back and take you to
be with me that you also may be where I am."*

JOHN 14:2–3 NIV

It boggles my mind to think about heaven, Lord.
And yet, You're already there, preparing a place
for me. Your plans for me don't just include the
here and now but the hereafter as well. This life of
mine is well thought out, isn't it? You haven't left
anything to chance. You've breathed new life into
my spirit so that I can walk out Your plan here on
earth and settle into my mansion in heaven once
this life is through. What an amazing and generous
Father You are! Amen.

Your Eye Is on Me

I will instruct you and teach you in the way you should go; I will counsel you with my eye upon you.

PSALM 32:8 ESV

What is it like, Lord, to sit in heaven and watch over Your children on earth? I would imagine it's like watching toddlers at play sometimes. What a patient Father You are! It's remarkable to think that You can see all of us at once: billions of people on Planet Earth, and Your eyes see all. You've also crafted specific plans for each of us, and You're always close by to make sure those plans come to fruition—even when we get off course. If we wander from the path, You're right there to lead us back again. What a loving Father You are. Thanks for watching over us. Amen.

SECTION THREE:
TAILORED FOR ME

*"For I know the plans I have for you," declares
the LORD, "plans to prosper you and not to harm
you, plans to give you hope and a future."*

JEREMIAH 29:11 NIV

Picture a mother with multiple children. She's planning a birthday party for her youngest. This loving mama knows what flavor of cake her little one likes best, which games will tickle his fancy, and which friends to invite. She's even crafted the perfect superhero theme for the event. She knows him so very well. The same is true with our heavenly Father. God has hand-tailored His plans for each of us. Think about that for a moment: He knows each of us so well that a generic plan won't work. It must be individualized. The plan He has laid out for your neighbor's life won't work for you. And the plan He has for you won't work for your child or grandchild. The intricate makings of our being are so clear to the Lord that He took the time to design something tailor-made. What a diligent and remarkable God we serve!

Good, Not Evil

You prepare a meal for me in front of my enemies.
PSALM 23:5 NCV

I wish the word *enemies* had never been invented, Father. I know, I know—You didn't come up with such a divisive notion. Your enemy, Satan, did. I've experienced division in my life, Lord, and it doesn't feel good. Not one little bit. But it brings me great comfort to know that You are preparing a table before me in the presence of the very people who rise up against me. This is part of Your great plan for my life, to guard me from those who would seek to do me harm. I'm so grateful for Your protection, Father! Amen.

Walking Out His Plan

I can do all things through Christ,
because he gives me strength.

PHILIPPIANS 4:13 NCV

Because I know Your plans are tailor-made for me, I can rest easy in the notion that You'll get me from point A to point B. In fact, You'll get me all the way through. You know how my feet move. You know how my thoughts ramble. You know how my ideas percolate. There's not a person on Planet Earth who knows me like You do and certainly no one capable of breathing strength into my weary bones when I feel like giving up. I submit myself to Your plans, Father, and thank You for the energy You're pouring into me today. Amen.

Straightened Paths

Trust in the LORD with all your heart and lean not on your own understanding; in all your ways submit to him, and he will make your paths straight.

PROVERBS 3:5–6 NIV

Okay, I'll admit it, Lord. When I make plans, they zigzag all over the place. Oh, initially they don't. I start off on the straight and narrow, but as I go along, things get a little crazy. Before I know it, what looked like a step forward becomes a jog to the right. And what looked like a simple step toward a goal becomes a complicated, dizzying journey I'm completely unprepared for. I'm so excited about the fact that You're a path straightener. Whew! You take my zigzags and turn them into a sensible road, one I can easily navigate with Your help. Thank You, Father. Amen.

What We Hope For

*Faith means being sure of the things we
hope for and knowing that something
is real even if we do not see it.*

HEBREWS 11:1 NCV

A good father knows his children. He knows not just their outward appearance but their longings and desires. He knows what little Johnny is hoping to unwrap under the Christmas tree and that little Susie is looking forward to a Tinkerbell party. In short, he knows their hopes. The same is true with You, Father. You know the things I'm wishing and hoping for. You know when I'm hoping to get that next pay raise or new job. You can see into my heart when I'm longing to be a better parent or wife. You know what I'm hoping for. And I'm so grateful, Father! Amen.

A Tailored Witness

*"But you will receive power when the Holy
Spirit comes on you; and you will be my
witnesses in Jerusalem, and in all Judea and
Samaria, and to the ends of the earth."*

ACTS 1:8 NIV

Where have You called me to go, Lord? How can
I reach others for You? How can I share Your love,
Your plan of salvation, with those around me? I
know You've got specific places and people in mind.
You haven't placed me here, where I live and work
and play, by accident. You've hand-tailored my
surroundings and want me to reach others in my
community for You. Show me, Lord. Lead. Guide.
Empower. I want to be a witness for You, Father.
Amen.

Marked Out for Me

Therefore, since we are surrounded by such a great cloud of witnesses, let us throw off everything that hinders and the sin that so easily entangles. And let us run with perseverance the race marked out for us.

HEBREWS 12:1 NIV

I can see it now, Lord. I'm at the starting block, just before a big race. A gunshot splits the air and I take off, light as a feather. Except this race is my life, and You're the One who has marked it out, just for me. A turn to the right, a turn to the left—You've left clear signals at the forks in the road. How grateful I am that You took the time to mark my path. As I aim myself toward You, I will keep my eye on the prize, Father. With a grateful heart, I run. Amen.

Desire Giver

Take delight in the LORD, and he will
give you the desires of your heart.

PSALM 37:4 NIV

How You love to surprise and delight me, Father!
Because You know me so well, You know the
little things that will bring a smile to my face. The
hidden desires of my heart—the things that even
my closest friends and loved ones don't know—are
crystal clear to You. And You love to fulfill those
desires in ways that only You can. I get a little giddy
when I think about how much You love me, Lord.
My greatest desire in the world is to know and love
You more. Praise You, Father. Amen.

Called to Shine

*"You are the light of the world. A town built on a hill
cannot be hidden. Neither do people light a lamp and
put it under a bowl. Instead they put it on its stand,
and it gives light to everyone in the house. In the same
way, let your light shine before others, that they may
see your good deeds and glorify your Father in heaven."*

MATTHEW 5:14–16 NIV

You've called me to shine Your light, Lord. That's an
important part of Your plan for my life. Sometimes
I feel the pressure of this too keenly. I want to be
the best witness for You that I can be. I don't want
my light to be a distraction to others; I want it
to guide them to You. But I'm so flawed, Father.
I make mistakes. Some days I'm like a flickering
candle, about to burn out. Thank You for giving me
multiple chances to shine, Lord. Light the flame
once again, I pray. Amen.

Understanding His Will

*Therefore do not be foolish, but understand
what the will of the Lord is.*

EPHESIANS 5:17 ESV

Lord, I remember how as a child I didn't always understand my parents' decisions. They asked things of me that made no sense. Now, as an adult, I understand that their desires for me were good, not evil. It's the same with You, Father. Though I might not always understand Your will in the moment, You make things crystal clear to me on the opposite side. May I always seek to understand Your will, Lord, even when the road ahead appears difficult to navigate. Amen.

Forgetting What Lies Behind

I do not mean that I am already as God wants me to be. I have not yet reached that goal, but I continue trying to reach it and to make it mine. Christ wants me to do that, which is the reason he made me his. Brothers and sisters, I know that I have not yet reached that goal, but there is one thing I always do. Forgetting the past and straining toward what is ahead, I keep trying to reach the goal and get the prize for which God called me through Christ to the life above.

PHILIPPIANS 3:12–14 NCV

I tend to crane my neck, Lord, keeping an eye on what's just happened as I plow forward. Help me to keep my focus on You, Father. Knowing You're in charge, knowing You have plans for me, helps me forget the things I've experienced and focus solely on You. Now that's a great perspective, Lord! Amen.

Your Eyes Saw

My frame was not hidden from you when I was made in the secret place, when I was woven together in the depths of the earth. Your eyes saw my unformed body; all the days ordained for me were written in your book before one of them came to be.

PSALM 139:15—16 NIV

It's so fascinating to think that You knew me even before I was born, Lord. Wow! When I was in my mother's womb, You kept careful watch. Even then, You knew who I would become, where I would live, whose lives I would impact. Thank You for calling me even from before my birth, Father! If my mother could trust You with the intimate details of my birth, surely I can trust You with the plans You have for my life. Amen.

Known by God

*"Before I formed you in the womb I knew you,
and before you were born I consecrated you;
I appointed you a prophet to the nations."*

JEREMIAH 1:5 ESV

Not only did You keep careful watch over me in the womb, Lord, but (like You did for Jeremiah) You consecrated me—set me apart—to do special things for You. What an amazing revelation, to know that I was called, chosen, and set apart even when my very bones were forming! How special are Your plans for my life, Father, that You took the time to set them in motion even before I drew my first breath. You are truly remarkable, Lord! Amen.

His Purpose Will Stand

*Many are the plans in the mind of a man, but
it is the purpose of the LORD that will stand.*

PROVERBS 19:21 ESV

You're the reason, Lord. You're the reason I'm still plowing forward. It's Your plans, Your goals, Your energy, Your passion, Your holy calling on my life. I've planned a million things in my life, and few of them came to fruition. I had some degree of passion but was lacking the "reason." Without a purpose, plans are just plans. I'm discovering Your reason, even now, Father. You want me to reach others with the Gospel message. When I'm moving in that direction, Your purposes stand as straight and tall as arrows. But when I turn my eyes to self, I stumble and fall. Thank You for keeping me aright today, Lord, as I share Your love with all I meet! Amen.

That You May Proclaim

*But you are a chosen race, a royal priesthood, a holy
nation, a people for his own possession, that you
may proclaim the excellencies of him who called
you out of darkness into his marvelous light.*

1 PETER 2:9 ESV

I'll proclaim it, Lord! I'll shout it out from the
rooftop, in fact. You are a most excellent Father,
worthy of praise. Grow my boldness, Father, that
I might willingly share with all who need to know
that there is a God who can pull them out of dark
places and into marvelous light. If I don't work up
the courage to share, who will? You've called me
and set me apart for this very purpose, that I might
make this proclamation. So, today I will tell others
how amazing You are. Thank You for making me
a hope giver, Father. I want to be like You. Amen.

The Light Shines

The light shines in the darkness,
and the darkness has not overcome it.

JOHN 1:5 ESV

I've been in situations that felt hopeless, Lord. It was almost as if the light had gone out and I was surrounded by utter darkness. Whenever I've been that low, any glimmer of daylight served to bring hope. Now I see that You're the One who opens the eyes of my heart. You bring light to dark situations. You're the One who reminds me of the calling on my life, even when I'm in a low spot, because You know that a ripple of hope will wash over me at the reminder. I'm so glad these low places don't last long, Father. Thank You for bringing hope in my darkest hour. Amen.

The Hairs of My Head

*"And even the very hairs of
your head are all numbered."*

MATTHEW 10:30 NIV

My ability to remember details appears to be waning, Father. Sometimes it's all I can do to remember a friend's birthday or a bill that needs to be paid. The little things slip right by me at times. But You, Lord? You never forget. You're in the details, 100 percent. It boggles my mind to think that You've numbered the hairs of my head. (I lost a few just this morning, Father—but You already knew that!) Even in an ever-changing environment, You still keep track. Oh, to be more like You, Lord. Give me eyes to see (and take care of) the details in my life. Thank You in advance. Amen.

Twinkle, Twinkle

He determines the number of the
stars and calls them each by name.

PSALM 147:4 NIV

Lord, You don't just know the number of stars, You actually *determine* the number of stars. You decide where to place them, how big they should be—everything. And You care enough about each one that You take the time to give them names. I'm looking forward to hearing these names when I get to heaven. What fun that will be! You're definitely in the details, Father. Nothing slips by You. To say You care about the little things would be an understatement. If You care about them, I can only imagine how You must feel about us, Your kids. You've called us by name too and called us to shine just like those stars above. Today, may I shimmer as never before. Thanks for caring so much, Lord. Amen.

One Step, Two Steps

"Does he not see my ways
and count my every step?"

JOB 31:4 NIV

I haven't counted my steps since I was a child, Lord. I remember doing it, though, to gauge distance. Of course, my tiny strides were a far cry from the steps I take today. It's fascinating to realize something as small as a step is on Your mind. You have so many other things to keep up with, Father! But there You are, watching me go here and there and keeping track of every step I take. May every move I make bring me closer to You, Lord. I don't want to waste even one step. I want every last one to count and to make a difference for Your kingdom. Use me, Lord, I pray. Amen.

Too Wonderful

*Such knowledge is too wonderful
for me, too lofty for me to attain.*

PSALM 139:6 NIV

So many things seem over my head, Lord. They are above me. When it comes to Your ways, Your Word, Your plans, I guess that's a good thing. If I understood Your ways, if I could comprehend the things You comprehend, then my need for You would be very small, wouldn't it? Oh, but I do need You, Father, and not just because of my lack of understanding. I stand in awe of who You are, Lord, and gaze on Your greatness with awe and wonder. You are too wonderful, Father! Amen.

Each One, Chosen

But in fact God has placed the parts in the body,
every one of them, just as he wanted them to be.
1 CORINTHIANS 12:18 NIV

You picked me, Lord! Of all the people in the world (and there are billions), You handpicked me to be a member of the family. It feels so good to be wanted. Needed. Loved. Thank You for arranging Your family across this great big globe as one unit. I have brothers and sisters as far as the eye can see. I need them—and they need me. Together, we are an unstoppable force in You, Lord. Praise You for that. Amen.

SECTION FOUR:
GOD DECLARES A THING

*"For I know the plans I have for you," declares
the LORD, "plans to prosper you and not to harm
you, plans to give you hope and a future."*

JEREMIAH 29:11 NIV

When the Creator God speaks, the whole earth
listens. His declarations are promises that we can
count on. Those promises are weighty and will
stand the test of time. They are His covenant to us.
We can take His Word to the bank. How powerful
are the words of the Lord. And what a wonderful
lesson for us as well. Our words carry weight too—
both for good and evil. There is power in the spoken
word. What will you declare today? Speak life over
every situation and watch as God moves.

You Speak to Me

"Have I not commanded you? Be strong and courageous. Do not be afraid; do not be discouraged, for the LORD your God will be with you wherever you go."

JOSHUA 1:9 NIV

They are the age-old questions, Lord: How can I hear Your voice? Is it really still and small, or are Your words booming, earthshaking? Can I hear You in the cries of a newborn or in the stillness of a stream trickling over rocks? Will I find Your thoughts in the Bible and carved on my heart? Truth is, I can hear only if my spiritual ears are opened, so today I offer them to You. Speak, Lord, in any way You choose. Bolster my courage. Lift my heart. Whisper, "Attagirl," like only You can. I'm listening, Father. Ears wide open. Amen.

Fullness of Life

*May you experience the love of Christ, though
it is too great to understand fully. Then you
will be made complete with all the fullness
of life and power that comes from God.*

EPHESIANS 3:19 NLT

I'm so grateful that You're speaking words of life
to my heart, Father. There's so much negativity in
this world. Sometimes I think the enemy of my
soul works overtime to bring me down. But I won't
let him. I'll tune out his voice and listen only to
what You're saying. What's that? Oh, You want me
to know that I have purpose, that my life is going
to be rich and full? I'm grateful for the reminder,
Lord! Praise You for speaking words of abundant
life. Amen.

Spoken into Existence

In the beginning God created the
heavens and the earth.

GENESIS 1:1 NIV

Father, I get it! You spoke the world (and everything in it) into existence. Your words brought even the tiniest ladybug to life. Before I was born, You spoke me into existence and knew the paths my life would take. Now, Father, You're teaching me to speak things into existence, to follow the pattern You've set for me. I can look at the situations in my life and speak words of life over them. When I do, the same creative power flows forth. Thank You, Lord, for the ability to speak life. Amen.

You Say I Can Overcome

*"I have told you all this so that you may have
peace in me. Here on earth you will have
many trials and sorrows. But take heart,
because I have overcome the world."*

JOHN 16:33 NLT

I don't always feel like an overcomer, Lord. So
many times I just want to crawl into a hole and
hide away, to give up completely. But You won't let
me! You just keep saying "You can do this, girl,"
followed by "Trust Me" and "Let Me lead you every
step of the way." I'm listening to those words of
encouragement today, Father. I really need them.
You're an overcomer, and I'm created in Your image,
which means I'm an overcomer too. I'll stand in that
knowledge today, Lord. Amen.

You Make Precious Promises

And because of his glory and excellence, he has given us great and precious promises. These are the promises that enable you to share his divine nature and escape the world's corruption caused by human desires.

2 PETER 1:4 NLT

I love listening when You speak, Lord, especially when You reiterate the promises found in Your Word. Oh, how I love them! You've promised never to leave me or forsake me. You've promised to send the Holy Spirit to comfort me in times of need. You've promised that You will meet all my needs according to Your riches in glory. Through these and hundreds of other promises, I see glimpses of Your divine nature. Thank You that Your promises are true. Amen.

You Say I Can Succeed

"Keep this Book of the Law always on your lips; meditate on it day and night, so that you may be careful to do everything written in it. Then you will be prosperous and successful."

JOSHUA 1:8 NIV

The world is full of cheerleaders. I hear them all the time, Lord. They tell me I can get rich quick, that I can lose twenty pounds in a month, that I can lower my interest rate on my credit card and save lots of money. These "cheers" are hyped up and don't ring true. But You, Lord? I love it when You cheer me on! You tell me I can succeed, that I can prosper. You don't offer any get-rich-quick schemes (thank goodness). Instead, You tell me that my success lies in my relationship with You. I'll stick with Your words, Father, that I might experience Your version of success. Amen.

You Speak with Authority

Then Jesus came to them and said, "All authority
in heaven and on earth has been given to me."

MATTHEW 28:18 NIV

All authority. All. What an amazing and bold declaration, Lord! There is no one beside You. No one to ask. No one to approach. No one to beg. You are the be-all and end-all, Father, and Your words (both over my life and over this universe) carry weight. With You, Lord, I can say, "The buck stops here," and mean it. "Whom have I in heaven but you?" (Psalm 73:25 NIV). No one, Father! You are enough. I submit myself to Your holy authority and bend my ear toward heaven, ready to hear Your responses to all of life's questions. Amen.

You Tell Me to Ask, Seek, Knock

"So I say to you: Ask and it will be given to you; seek and you will find; knock and the door will be opened to you."

LUKE 11:9 NIV

You ask me to take action, Father. You want me to ask, so I come to You boldly, my request made known. You ask me to seek, so, Lord, I seek Your will—and Your way—with my whole heart. Not my will but Yours be done, Father. You ask me to knock, so here I stand, Lord, my knuckles rap-rap-rapping on the door of Your heart. I'm engaged in the process and will hover close, asking, seeking, knocking as long as it takes. I'm so grateful for the open doors You are placing in front of me, even now. Amen.

You Say I Can Shine Like a Star

"Those who are wise will shine like the brightness of the heavens, and those who lead many to righteousness, like the stars for ever and ever."

DANIEL 12:3 NIV

I must confess: sometimes my candle feels more like a dying ember than a shining star, Lord. I reach the burnt-out stage pretty quickly. Even on the best of days, I don't always shine like I should. Thank You for the reminder that You've called me to shine like the brightness of the firmament. I can only do this if I'm a reflection of You, and that's my chief aim from this moment on. It's not my glory, Father. It's not my light. It's all You, Lord. May I be a beautiful reflection of You. Amen.

You're Not a Human Being

"God is not human, that he should lie, not a human being, that he should change his mind. Does he speak and then not act? Does he promise and not fulfill?"

NUMBERS 23:19 NIV

Your Word is truthful in all situations, Lord. I can trust that what You say will be fulfilled. You're not like the people I've known who say one thing but mean another. Sometimes humans (myself included) have great intentions when they make promises, but they don't follow through. Some say, "Sure, I'll be there for you," and then they're not. But You're not like that, Father. Every promise You've ever spoken (either in Your Word or whispered in my ear) is solid-gold truth. I'm so grateful. Amen.

Your Words Are Exalted

He says, "Be still, and know that I am
God; I will be exalted among the nations,
I will be exalted in the earth."

PSALM 46:10 NIV

Lord, Your Word is exalted above all. Even a decree from the greatest ruler on earth can't compare. The opinions of Hollywood stars don't even come close. Even the finest teachers and educators can't speak with the same level of authority that You have. Thank You for the reminder that all I have to do is be still and know that You are God. When I'm in that position of submission, You are exalted in all the earth. Oh, what a magnificent Father You are. Be exalted forever, Lord! Amen.

All Things Are Possible

And Jesus said to him, "'If you can'! All things are possible for one who believes."

MARK 9:23 ESV

I've pondered this verse long and hard, Lord. It's remarkable to think that *all* things are possible if only I believe. I know, of course, that *all* refers to the things that are inside of Your will and Your plan for my life. But how remarkable to know that I play a role in seeing these things come to pass. There's power in believing. Today I choose to believe that Your plans for my life are good. I choose to believe that I have a hopeful future. If ever I doubt, Father, remind me afresh that all I have to do is believe. Amen.

A Lasting Promise

*"Heaven and earth will pass away,
but my words will not pass away."*

MATTHEW 24:35 ESV

So few things last, Lord. I buy a loaf of bread and it's hard within a week. A jug of milk? It's good for seven to ten days at best. Even my vehicles have let me down sooner than I'd hoped. Things in this life just aren't designed to last forever. That's one reason I take such comfort in the idea that Your words aren't just for the here and now (like that loaf of bread) but for ten years from now and even into eternity. It's hard to imagine "forever," Father. I'm trying to wrap my mind around it. But I'm so glad to know that You're a "forever" kind of friend, One I can trust from here on out. Thank You for this declaration that Your words will never pass away. Praise You for that. Amen.

Be Still

*"The LORD will fight for you;
you need only to be still."*

EXODUS 14:14 NIV

I'm so busy, Lord! There are days when I'm rushing here and there and barely pause to catch my breath. On those days, I often forget to meet with You. Sometimes, in the craziness, I also forget that You've already made plans for me. I strike out on my own without asking Your opinion. Thank You for the reminder that pausing to be with You is the first step to a great day. Teach me to be still in Your presence, to wait on You. I'll need a lot of reminding, Lord, but don't give up on me. What a blessing to know that You will fight for me, if I will only slow down long enough to let You. Amen.

Long Life

"Honor your father and your mother,
so that you may live long in the land
the LORD your God is giving you."

EXODUS 20:12 NIV

I love this promise, Lord! Thank You for this declaration. If I honor my father and mother (and the other elders You've placed in my life), my days will be long. Show me how to respect those You've placed in authority over me. May Your plans for our relationship shine through, even during the tough seasons. And, Father, show me how to lead those You've entrusted to my care (my children or others I teach and tend to). I want them to know the blessing of a good, long life too. May we all, as Your children, learn from You. You're the ultimate Father, and we live to bring honor and glory to Your name. Amen.

Written on Their Hearts

"This is the covenant I will make with the people of Israel after that time," declares the LORD. "I will put my law in their minds and write it on their hearts. I will be their God, and they will be my people."

JEREMIAH 31:33 NIV

I get overwhelmed when I think of how personal Your plans for my life are, God. The covenants that You've made with me are, in many ways, like the laws You wrote on the hearts of Your people in Old Testament times. When You take the time to write something on my heart, I know You mean it. You won't go back on Your word. We're talking about a permanent etching here, one that sticks. I'm completely humbled to think You would care enough about me to write something so personal, just for me. Bless You, Father! Amen.

Through the Waters

"When you pass through the waters, I will be with you; and when you pass through the rivers, they will not sweep over you. When you walk through the fire, you will not be burned; the flames will not set you ablaze."

ISAIAH 43:2 NIV

Lord, there have been so many "deep water" situations in my life. Many times, I felt as if I would drown. I nearly lost sight of Your plans for my life. "Tomorrow" felt like an elusive dream. Thank You for the reminder that the things I'm walking through will not consume me. I won't drown, even with the swirling floodwaters threatening to take me down. You have declared this over my life, Father, and I am grateful for Your assurance that I can make it through any situation, good or bad. Amen.

Your Spirit Is on Me

*The Spirit of the Lord God is on me, because the
Lord has chosen me to bring good news to poor
people. He has sent me to heal those with a sad
heart. He has sent me to tell those who are being
held and those in prison that they can go free.*

ISAIAH 61:1 NLV

I'm overwhelmed when I think about this verse,
Lord. What an amazing declaration. You have
poured out Your Spirit on me and filled me from
the inside out. You have anointed me to reach my
little corner of the world. You have called me to
do great things for Your kingdom. What specific
plans You've crafted for my life, Father. Your
calling is irrevocable. You send me out to those in
bondage to proclaim good news, and (even though
I'm frightened at times) I choose to go. Use me,
Father. With Your Spirit on me, I can do anything.
Hallelujah! Amen.

Train Up a Child

Direct your children onto the right path,
and when they are older, they will not leave it.

PROVERBS 22:6 NLT

Oh, Lord, of all Your many declarations, this is one of my favorites! It brings such peace to hear that my children will (eventually) walk the right path. There are days when I wonder, Father. Some have turned to their own way, bringing this scripture into question in my mind. Oh, but how wonderful to realize that "when they are older" (which could be any time now, since we're all aging rapidly), they will not leave it. I'm hanging on to that promise, Father. Amen.

I Declare!

If you openly declare that Jesus is Lord and believe in your heart that God raised him from the dead, you will be saved. For it is by believing in your heart that you are made right with God, and it is by openly declaring your faith that you are saved.

ROMANS 10:9–10 NLT

Lord, Your declarations are powerful. But You're teaching me that mine can be powerful too. Today, I openly declare that Jesus Christ is Lord. I choose to believe that You raised Him from the dead, Father. Because I truly believe what I'm declaring, I know that I'm made right with You. What an amazing declaration. It has truly changed my life—and my eternity. All praise to You! Amen.

SECTION FIVE:
"PLANS TO PROSPER YOU"

*"For I know the plans I have for you," declares
the LORD, "plans to prosper you and not to harm
you, plans to give you hope and a future."*

JEREMIAH 29:11 NIV

The Gospels provide a beautiful and encouraging message of prosperity but not necessarily the version you'll find on TV. God wants us to prosper, even as our soul prospers. Think about that for a moment. When our soul (i.e., our heart and mind) is doing well, everything else in our lives will follow suit. God longs for us to prosper in our thought life, our emotions, and our relationships. He longs for that same spirit of prosperity to spill over into our workplace and our neighborhoods. And while He might not cause us to become millionaires, God is very interested in our provision. He will meet every need.

Prospering in the Valley

Even when I walk through the darkest valley,
I will not be afraid, for you are close beside me.
Your rod and your staff protect and comfort me.

PSALM 23:4 NLT

I've walked through some dark valleys, Father. I know You were there, because I sensed the times You carried me. I don't claim to understand the difficult seasons, Lord. I wish they were fewer and farther between. But there is comfort in knowing that the valleys are easier to navigate now that I understand I'm not alone. You can even show me how to prosper (i.e., do well) during hard seasons. Thank You for never leaving me, and please show me how to be a better friend to those who are walking through valleys today. Amen.

A Very Full Cup

LORD, you alone are my inheritance,
my cup of blessing.
PSALM 16:5 NLT

I know the age-old question, Lord: Do you see the glass as half-empty or half-full? My answer to this question determines how I view the situations I face. Oh, how I love the idea that Your plans to prosper me include a cup that's overflowing with blessings. I won't be looking for it at the bank, Father, but rather in the tiniest details of my life. You have blessed me with friends, mentors, a job, health, and so many other things. You meet my every need, Father. I am well taken care of. Thank You for filling my cup to the top, Lord. Amen.

Prospering in the Details

And we know that in all things God
works for the good of those who love him,
who have been called according to his purpose.

ROMANS 8:28 NIV

I don't always remember that all things work together for good. Sometimes I get lost in the details, in the nitty-gritty. Oh, but You've reminded me that I can prosper, even in the minutiae. When the day is overwhelmingly busy. When the car breaks down. When the kids won't stop fighting. When the boss is pushing me to recheck my work. Even then, Lord, You're there. Your plan to bring prosperity to my life often takes me to places where I'm inundated with details. But there You are, Father, in the midst of them all. How grateful I am! Amen.

A Watered Garden

"And the Lord will guide you continually and satisfy your desire in scorched places and make your bones strong; and you shall be like a watered garden, like a spring of water, whose waters do not fail."

ISAIAH 58:11 ESV

When I think about Your plans for my life, I get so excited, Lord! I don't know what's coming next, but that's half the adventure. I do know that You are tending to every detail, even in the scorched and dry seasons. You're pouring out fresh water, saturating everything with Your Spirit. This water won't fail me, even when I'm feeling parched. You will bring hope, life, and energy to every situation. I'm so grateful, Father. Amen.

Prospering: A Blessed Outcome

"But seek first his kingdom and his righteousness,
and all these things will be given to you as well."

MATTHEW 6:33 NIV

What a lesson this verse has been to me, Lord. I'm so quick to ask for Your blessings, but not as quick to seek Your kingdom first. Usually it's my kingdom I'm after! My desires and my will are usually top priority. Today I acknowledge that and ask for Your forgiveness. From now on, Father, may Your desires be mine as well. As I run hard after You, after Your will, I know that blessings will come. You desire to prosper me by meeting every need. But my motivation will be for You, Lord. Thanks for the timely reminder. Amen.

The Oil of Blessing

For harmony is as precious as the anointing oil that was poured over Aaron's head, that ran down his beard and onto the border of his robe.

PSALM 133:2 NLT

I get it, Lord. One of the ways You want to prosper me is to teach me to walk in harmony with others. When I choose to live this way, the benefits are as precious as fine oil. (I can almost smell it now!) It's not always easy to get along with folks (even inside the walls of my local church), but I love the idea that our unity causes a sweet-smelling fragrance that others will witness and want for themselves. I'm so grateful for Your oil of blessing, Father. Thank You for showing me how to bring honor to Your name through my relationships. Amen.

A Joyous Celebration

*"You will live in joy and peace. The mountains
and hills will burst into song, and the trees of
the field will clap their hands! Where once there
were thorns, cypress trees will grow. Where nettles
grew, myrtles will sprout up. These events will
bring great honor to the LORD's name; they will
be an everlasting sign of his power and love."*

ISAIAH 55:12–13 NLT

Father, every day can be a celebration when I walk
in relationship with You! With my eyes tipped
upward toward You, how can my heart help but
sing? My focus on You brings joy. It brings peace,
even when things around me are swirling. And
if I need any reminders of what it's like to live in
holy celebration, all I need to do is look around at
nature. The very mountains are singing, even now.
Trees are clapping their hands in praise. I join them
in bringing honor to Your name, Father. Amen.

An Earnest Reward

And it is impossible to please God without faith. Anyone who wants to come to him must believe that God exists and that he rewards those who sincerely seek him.

HEBREWS 11:6 NLT

I've never been much for dieting, Lord. It's never fun to sacrifice things I love. Oh, but the rewards can be amazing. It's so much fun to look at before-and-after photos when I've dropped a few pounds. Is that how You feel sometimes, Lord? Do You look at my spiritual before-and-after photos and smile? (I hope I'm progressing in the right direction!) The rewards of seeking You are mine for the taking, but I don't serve You for what I can get out of it. I continue to grow in my relationship with You, Father, because I adore You. I want to please You in all that I do. Amen.

Fruit of the Spirit

But the fruit of the Spirit is love, joy, peace,
forbearance, kindness, goodness, faithfulness, gentleness
and self-control. Against such things there is no law.

GALATIANS 5:22–23 NIV

I see how it is, Father—You want to prosper me from the inside out. What good would it do to lavish gifts on me if my heart wasn't in the right place? I would be like a spoiled child, demanding favors but never checking my attitude. Instead, You prosper my soul. You teach me how to live in peace. In joy. Exhibiting kindness, even to those who've hurt me. You prosper me by showing me how to remain faithful, even when I don't feel like it. And You're teaching me self-control, every step of the way. I love prospering from the inside out, Lord. Thank You! Amen.

Supernatural Strength

He gives strength to the weary and
increases the power of the weak.

ISAIAH 40:29 NIV

It's fascinating to think about, Lord. Your plans for my life are fully in place, even when I'm exhausted, even when I don't feel like I can put one foot in front of the other. After all, I reach the end of myself pretty quickly, as You well know. I hit a wall. During those times, I can't think clearly, can't move forward. Then You come along. You miraculously give me energy. It comes on me in a supernatural way and even surprises me. With Your strength, I'm able to do more than ever before. Or, I should say that You're able to do more through me. Today, I give You my weariness. I ask You to breathe on me, Holy Spirit, and energize me. Make me a vibrant channel You can flow through. I submit myself to that process. Amen.

All Hope and Peace

May the God of hope fill you with all joy and
peace as you trust in him, so that you may overflow
with hope by the power of the Holy Spirit.
ROMANS 15:13 NIV

Of all the ways You promise to prosper me, Lord,
this is one of my favorites. You are the God of all
hope and peace. Wow. What good would it do to
have everything I'd ever wished for, everything I'd
ever dreamed of, if I didn't have hope and peace?
Those two things are critical for a prosperous life.
And You don't just dole out hope by the teaspoonful,
Father. You pour it over me like an ocean wave! I
can overflow, Lord, as I trust in You. Today I choose
to do just that. Amen.

An Eternal Perspective

*Then Peter said, "Silver or gold I do not have,
but what I do have I give you. In the name
of Jesus Christ of Nazareth, walk."*

ACTS 3:6 NIV

When people think of the word *prosper*, their
thoughts often shift to money, lottery tickets, gold
coins, jewels, fancy clothes, luxury vehicles, and so
on. But You are changing our thinking about this
word, Lord, and I love it. You're giving us an eternal
perspective. We can't take money with us when we
die. Neither can we take fine jewels nor any of the
other things that the world considers prosperous.
Instead of focusing on those things, today I ask that
You give me an eternal perspective. Silver and gold
have I none. (Well, very little anyway.) But I have
a heavenly perspective that is giving me courage to
walk into tomorrow with confidence. Praise You,
Father! Amen.

Abundant Life

"The thief comes only to steal and kill and destroy. I came that they may have life and have it abundantly."

JOHN 10:10 ESV

I will never have to doubt Your motivation, Lord. You've stated it so clearly in this verse. Your heart for Your children is life—and abundant life, at that. You're not interested in settling for an ordinary, humdrum existence, one day dragging to the next. No, You want to stir us up, to create an adventurous road, to use us in miraculous ways. Wow! You sent Your Son, Jesus, the Life Giver, to show us how to live. May we learn from His example, Father, so that our impact on this world will be a thing of beauty. Amen.

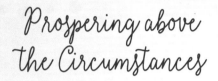

Prospering above the Circumstances

But those who hope in the LORD will renew
their strength. They will soar on wings like
eagles; they will run and not grow weary,
they will walk and not be faint.

ISAIAH 40:31 NIV

So many times, Lord, I live *under* my circumstances. I let them weigh me down. They dictate whether I move forward. Many times, I remain frozen in place, convinced there's no point in trying. You've asked me to live *above* my circumstances, not below them. With Your help, I can actually soar as free as an eagle. What a hopeful image that paints in my mind! Instead of allowing my challenges to cause weariness, I'll mount up with wings energized by Your Spirit—and off I'll go, stronger than ever. Thank You for lifting me, Lord. Amen.

Every Need Met

And my God will meet all your needs according
to the riches of his glory in Christ Jesus.

PHILIPPIANS 4:19 NIV

Oh, how I love the word *every*, Lord. You don't just want to meet my financial needs. You don't just long to meet my physical needs. You're not going to stop until *every* need is met. What peace this brings! When my needs are emotional, You're there. When I'm in need of provision, You've got it covered. There's not a need I could name that You haven't already provided for. Wow. It boggles my mind when I think about the "everys" in my life. You've got 'em, Lord, and I'm so grateful. Amen.

Every Good and Perfect Gift

*Whatever is good and perfect is a gift
coming down to us from God our Father,
who created all the lights in the heavens. He
never changes or casts a shifting shadow.*

JAMES 1:17 NLT

Sometimes I forget, Lord. I forget that my belongings didn't really come from a store. My income doesn't really come from an employer. My home doesn't really come from a bank or mortgage company. All good things come from You. If it's good, if it's for my benefit, it's all You, Father. And it's all because of Your great love for us, Your kids. You desire to meet every need. May we never forget that our efforts, though good, would never be enough, if not for Your provision and Your great love. Praise You, Lord. Amen.

Eternal Life: The Ultimate Gift

*For God did not send his Son into the
world to condemn the world, but to
save the world through him.*

JOHN 3:17 NIV

So many people in this world are quick to cut me down, Lord. They pass judgment. Bring condemnation. But not You. You're the last one to chop me to bits. In fact, You went out of Your way to do the opposite! Through the gift of Your Son, You've saved me. Sure, You want me to live a godly life. Jesus showed me how to do that— through His actions, His words, His love for others. May I be ever grateful for the ultimate gift from the God of the universe. Amen.

As My Soul Prospers

Dear friend, I pray that you may enjoy good health and that all may go well with you, even as your soul is getting along well.

3 JOHN 1:2 NIV

I've walked through dark seasons in the past, and You've seen me through, Lord. There were times when my heart was so broken, I wondered if it would ever heal. My dark days even affected my health, setting me on a downward spiral of sorts. It's hard to believe I've come so far. I thank You for the healing work You've done inside of me, Father, and I look ahead with excitement. When my heart is healthy and whole (i.e., prosperous), my body will follow suit. I can walk with renewed optimism, which greatly affects my health. I want to be completely whole in You, Lord. Amen.

No Lack

*The LORD your God has blessed everything
you have done; he has protected you while you
traveled through this great desert. The LORD your
God has been with you for the past forty years,
and you have had everything you needed.*

DEUTERONOMY 2:7 NCV

I don't always get what I want, Lord, but You make
sure I always have what I need. Even during my
lean seasons, when the cupboard wasn't as full as I
would have liked, You managed to get me through.
No matter how many valleys I walk through, no
matter how many deserts I traverse, You'll provide
manna for the journey. I'll never come up short.
You're a God of provision. With You, I will always
have what I need. Thank You, Father. Amen.

Abounding in Love

*Lord, you are kind and forgiving and have
great love for those who call to you.*

PSALM 86:5 NCV

If anyone had told me I'd be this loved, Father, I'm
not sure I would have believed them. From the time
I was a little girl, I yearned for love. So many times,
I was disappointed. People act loving but turn on
a dime, their affections waning. You, Lord? You've
never changed. You were abounding in love the
day I met You and continue to pour out affections.
Even when I wander down the wrong road or make
mistakes, there You are, loving me still. Praise You
for Your goodness to me, Father. My soul prospers
because of Your great love. Amen.

SECTION SIX: "NOT TO HARM"

"For I know the plans I have for you," declares
the LORD, "plans to prosper you and not to harm
you, plans to give you hope and a future."

JEREMIAH 29:11 NIV

Most of us know what it feels like to have the rug
pulled out from underneath us. We're buzzing along
just fine, and then. . .*bam*. Down we go. Sometimes
those we love and trust turn out to be the culprits.
They bring us harm. They don't just yank the rug
out from under us, they steal the rug too. The pain
can be significant, particularly when it comes from
the hands of someone we thought we could trust.
God will never let us down like that. In Jeremiah
29:11, He promises to bring us good and not evil.
This doesn't mean we won't walk through seasons
of loss and devastation, but it brings comfort to
know that God's intentions for us are good. He will
never purposely bring harm to His kids.

Your Will Is Perfect

Do not be shaped by this world; instead be changed within by a new way of thinking. Then you will be able to decide what God wants for you; you will know what is good and pleasing to him and what is perfect.

ROMANS 12:2 NCV

Your Word tells me that I need to pray for Your will to be done, Father. It's not always easy, I'll admit. When I ponder the notion that I need to bend my will to Yours, I realize it all comes down to one word: *trust*. If I can really grab hold of the truth that You will never harm me, that You are only looking out for my good, then I can trust that Your will is perfect. Thinking like this is a new thing for me, I must admit. But I'm learning that Your will (even when it does not match my own) is good and pleasing and perfect! How could I say no to that? I trust You, Lord. Amen.

For My Sake

But he was wounded for the wrong we did; he
was crushed for the evil we did. The punishment,
which made us well, was given to him, and
we are healed because of his wounds.

ISAIAH 53:5 NCV

If I needed any additional proof that You want only good things for me, Father, I need look no further than Your Son. How sobering, to realize that He took the punishment for my sins. I deserved to be punished but received only good instead. It's remarkable to think that You would do anything for my sake. When I put this in perspective, Father, I realize that I should be doing everything for Your sake. What an amazing revelation. Today I commit myself to trying harder. May I focus more on Your will than my own, Lord. Help me? Amen.

Good-Gift Giver

"Which of you, if your son asks for bread, will give him a stone? Or if he asks for a fish, will give him a snake? If you, then, though you are evil, know how to give good gifts to your children, how much more will your Father in heaven give good gifts to those who ask him!"

MATTHEW 7:9–11 NIV

You give great gifts, Father. Walking with You is like Christmas 365 days a year. Your gifts are more fun to unwrap and last longer than any I've been given. I won't be returning any of them, either! They're hand-tailored, just for me. You know best how to deliver them and how to teach me to use them. If I have any problems, I go straight to the owner's manual (Your Word) for direction. Oh, how I've loved discovering all of these gifts, Lord. Thank You for entrusting them to me. I promise to use them for You. Amen.

More Than I Could Ask or Imagine

Now to him who is able to do immeasurably more than all we ask or imagine, according to his power that is at work within us, to him be glory in the church and in Christ Jesus throughout all generations, for ever and ever! Amen.

EPHESIANS 3:20–21 NIV

I've always loved this verse, Lord! I'm a dreamer with a vivid imagination, as You well know, so I'm always asking for over-the-top things. It's so fun to realize that You are able to do immeasurably more than all I could ask or think. You do it all by Your power, Father, not mine. (This is a very good thing, as I'm limited in my abilities.) Your plans for me include fun, over-the-top things, because You're a creative God. I can't wait to see what You have in store. Looking forward to it, Father. Amen.

For My Peace

"Peace I leave with you; my peace I give you. I do not give to you as the world gives. Do not let your hearts be troubled and do not be afraid."

JOHN 14:27 NIV

I'm glad that true peace comes from You, Lord, and not from the world around me. People are always telling me how to obtain their version of peace, but it never lasts long. Sometimes I feel so burdened by troubles that it's hard to clear my mind. Then You show up, Father, sweeping away the turmoil in my heart and offering hope that my situation can and will change. My favorite part of this verse is the word *leave*, Lord. You're leaving Your peace with me. It's not on loan—it's mine forever. What a generous God You are! I'm so grateful. Amen.

You've Shown the Way

He has shown you, O man, what is good; and what
does the LORD require of you but to do justly, to
love mercy, and to walk humbly with your God?

MICAH 6:8 NKJV

I never have to guess with You, Lord. You're a
terrific leader. Your Word, the Bible, gives me great
guidance. You also lead me as You gently whisper
directions in my ear. You nudge me forward with
life's circumstances, as well. Anytime I'm feeling
confused, You're right there, showing me the way.
Because You've done this so many millions of times
before, I know You'll do it again. And all You ask
in exchange is that I continue to walk with You,
living as You've shown me how to live, loving those
You've given me to love. Now that's a good deal,
Father! Thank You. Amen.

Perfect Peace

"You will keep him in perfect peace, whose mind is stayed on You, because he trusts in You."

ISAIAH 26:3 NKJV

I confess, Lord, my thoughts don't remain fixed, or still, very often. They ping-pong from place to place, problem to problem, incident to incident. They soar up and then down again. I'm like a kid on a roller coaster much of the time. One of the hardest challenges I've faced in my walk with You is slowing my mind long enough to actually "stay" on You. But I'm working on it, Father. I love this promise that You will keep my mind in perfect peace once I'm able to come into Your presence and shift my focus to You. As the storms around me calm, my trust grows. Help me with this, Father. I want to be fixed on You. Amen.

Steadfast

*Therefore, my beloved brethren, be
steadfast, immovable, always abounding
in the work of the Lord, knowing that
your labor is not in vain in the Lord.*

1 CORINTHIANS 15:58 NKJV

Father, this verse reminds me of how I feel when I
watch the news during a major storm and see those
reporters out in high winds. I'm always terrified
they'll blow over! Sometimes I'm afraid I'll blow
over too, and not just during stormy seasons. Life's
circumstances are overwhelming at times and
threaten to take me down. But Your Word tells me
that I can be immovable. Those winds won't topple
me. I know nothing will bring me harm when I
walk in Your strength, Father. Show me how to
remain steadfast, even when the storms of life
thunder overhead. Amen.

A Forever-After Journey

For the wages of sin is death, but the gift of God is eternal life in Christ Jesus our Lord.

ROMANS 6:23 NKJV

I love looking through a telescope, Lord, to the vast corners of this marvelous universe. It's an amazing thing, to see so far out into space. Oh, but how much farther, to see all the way into eternity. There's no telescope powerful enough. Your Word gives me amazing glimpses, though, and what I see gets me excited! You've got such joyous things planned for Your kids when we reach heaven. No tears. No crying. Just a forever-after journey with the King of kings and Lord of lords. Praise You for this amazing gift, Father. I can't wait to spend eternity with You. Amen.

Gently Leading

The LORD is my shepherd, I lack nothing. He
makes me lie down in green pastures, he leads me
beside quiet waters, he refreshes my soul. He guides
me along the right paths for his name's sake.

PSALM 23:1–3 NIV

What a gentle leader You are, Father! I've had earthly leaders who left something to be desired. They pushed too hard, asked too much, or insisted on their own way. But You? You're just the opposite, Lord. You're such a gentle and good shepherd. When I'm weary, You lead me beside still waters. When I'm ready to collapse, You point out places along the path where I can rest. Unlike most earthly leaders, You're more interested in me—in my well-being—than anything else. And yet somehow You manage to do it all for Your name's sake. I want to be that kind of leader, Lord. May I learn from Your amazing example. Amen.

A Strong Tower

The name of the LORD is a fortified tower;
the righteous run to it and are safe.

PROVERBS 18:10 NIV

I've scoped out my house, Lord, and know just where to go in case of an emergency. I've picked out the safest room, one where I can wait out the storms. There's another place I love to run to when spiritual storms hit. I sprint straight into Your presence. Not that I have to run very far. You're right next to me, after all. All I have to do is speak the name of Jesus and I'm cocooned in safety. Thank You, my Strong Tower, for always being a refuge. Nothing can harm me when I'm tucked away in that holy place. Praise You, Lord! Amen.

You Bring Me Forth as Gold

"But he knows the way that I take; when he has tested me, I will come forth as gold."

JOB 23:10 NIV

I'm beginning to understand the phrase *trial by fire*, Lord. It's not fun, going through the fire, but the result is pretty astounding! I'm like a beautiful golden ring, exquisitely shaped by the Master Artist. Best of all, the trial by fire purifies me and rids me of the things that drag me down. Your plans for me are so holy, Lord, so special, that they require me to be the best I can be. So purify my heart today, Father. Cleanse me from within. Shape me into Your image. Bring me from the furnace, a new woman of God, ready to do Your will. I submit myself to the process, Lord. Amen.

You Meet My Needs

"So do not worry, saying, 'What shall we eat?' or 'What shall we drink?' or 'What shall we wear?' For the pagans run after all these things, and your heavenly Father knows that you need them."

MATTHEW 6:31–32 NIV

Okay, I'll confess—this is a tough one for me at times, Lord. Sometimes worries slip in. I wonder about the bills. I question Your ability to provide for me. I get bound up with worry as I see my apparent lack. But with You, Father, there is no lack! Thank You for that reminder. I don't want to run after "stuff." You know what I need, and You'll make sure I have enough for each day. That's Your promise. You'll meet all of my needs—emotional, financial, spiritual, and physical. You've got me covered, Lord, and I'm so grateful. Praise You. Amen.

You Intercede for Me

*And he who searches our hearts knows the mind of
the Spirit, because the Spirit intercedes for God's
people in accordance with the will of God.*

ROMANS 8:27 NIV

Father, I know what it's like to intercede for
someone. I've gone to bat for loved ones many times
over. When I feel passionately about a situation,
I'm happy to come out swinging. It's amazing
to me that You search my heart and Your Spirit
intercedes for me, according to Your will. Even
now, intercession is taking place for millions across
this globe as You search hearts from continent to
continent. Remarkable! There are things happening
in the spiritual realm that we cannot see or hear,
but I'm thrilled to know You are for us, not against
us. Thank You for caring and for interceding on our
behalf. Amen.

Your Unfailing Love

When I said, "My foot is slipping," your unfailing love, LORD, supported me. When anxiety was great within me, your consolation brought me joy.

PSALM 94:18–19 NIV

How many times have I slipped on proverbial banana peels, Lord? Dozens! I'm walking along just fine, and then down I go. It brings great comfort to know You catch me when I fall. You're the King of soft landings! You're there for me because You love me. (This I have experienced and know to be true.) Even in my deepest troubles, You've held me upright and put a smile on my face. Father, You must have big plans for me. You've kept me upright so that I can keep moving forward with You. Praise You for Your great love. Amen.

Your Works Abound

O Lord, how many are Your works!
You made them all in wisdom. The
earth is full of what You have made.

PSALM 104:24 NLV

Not a day goes by that I don't marvel at Your creation, Lord. The lustrous blue sky. The curving peaks of a mountain range. An infant's joyous smile. A butterfly, its wings spread in flight. A hummingbird alighting on a feeder. Signs of Your creative handiwork abound. If You took the time to pour such thought into even the smallest of things, then I know You've spent even more effort designing me. And You've designed me for greatness, Father. I pray that my works will abound, as well. May I do great and mighty things for Your kingdom, Lord. Amen.

You Know My Path

When my spirit had grown weak within me,
You knew my path. They have hidden a
trap for me in the way where I walk.

PSALM 142:3 NLV

Not everyone is for me. I know this, Lord. There are people who would rather not see me succeed. They want to knock me off my path. I won't let them get me down, though, or send me veering in the wrong direction. Even when they weaken my resistance, I'll keep my focus on You. You're the only one who knows the direction this road is leading. How could I help but trust You? No matter how many traps are set, You'll guide me safely past them so that I can continue to grow in You. Praise You for that, Lord. Amen.

Shining-Greatness
Is on Its Way

I am sure that our suffering now cannot be
compared to the shining-greatness
that He is going to give us.
ROMANS 8:18 NLV

I'm trying to imagine what Your shining-greatness will look like, Lord. I've already tasted of Your goodness, shared in Your blessings, and witnessed miracles. I've spent quiet, intimate time in Your presence and have marveled that You continue to woo someone as flawed as me. There's really more to come, Lord? I can hardly wait. When I'm in the middle of a rough patch, please remind me that my suffering is only temporary. It cannot be compared with the glory around the bend, Father. I can only imagine what You've got in store. Praise You! Amen.

You Hear. . .and Act

"If My people who are called by My name put away
their pride and pray, and look for My face, and turn
from their sinful ways, then I will hear from heaven.
I will forgive their sin, and will heal their land."

2 CHRONICLES 7:14 NLV

Are You waiting right now, Lord? Waiting for me to pack away my pride, turn to You, and seek Your face? Are You waiting for Your people to turn from the things that have bound them, to cry out to You, and to ask for forgiveness of sins? I can't even imagine what it must feel like on Your end, Lord, as You wait for Your children to do the right thing. You're such a gracious God! The minute You hear our call, You spring into action. And You don't stop there. You're so motivated by our call that You forgive our sin and bring healing to our land. Father, forgive me for the many times I've kept You waiting. I turn to You today. Amen.

Live Together with Him

But since we belong to the day, let us be sober, putting on faith and love as a breastplate, and the hope of salvation as a helmet. For God did not appoint us to suffer wrath but to receive salvation through our Lord Jesus Christ. He died for us so that, whether we are awake or asleep, we may live together with him.

1 THESSALONIANS 5:8–10 NIV

I know what it's like to live in a crowded house, Lord. I've had to share space with others and it's not always comfortable. But sharing space with You? That's a privilege! When I said yes to Your Son, You swept me into Your home and welcomed me to dwell with You. I'm honored to live with You, Father. Thanks for throwing out the welcome mat! Amen.

SECTION SEVEN:
THE HOPE GIVER

*"For I know the plans I have for you," declares
the LORD, "plans to prosper you and not to harm
you, plans to give you hope and a future."*

JEREMIAH 29:11 NIV

So many things we do in life (good or bad) come
down to one word: *motivation*. If our motivations
our pure, our actions will follow. Isn't it comforting
to realize that we will never have to question God's
motivations? His heart for us is always good. What
is His motivation for His carefully laid plans for us?
To bring us hope. Picture the hand of God like a
giant ladle in a pot of soup, stirring, stirring, stirring.
He longs to stir up hope in hopeless situations. He
longs to whisper words of hope when we're feeling
lost in a sea of blackness. His plans are always
meant to encourage, to uplift, to bring hope for the
journey. What an amazing hope giver our God is!

You Are Rejoicing over Me

"The LORD your God is with you, the Mighty Warrior who saves. He will take great delight in you; in his love he will no longer rebuke you, but will rejoice over you with singing."

ZEPHANIAH 3:17 NIV

How could I remain in the pits when I read a verse like this? I can picture You now, Lord, singing and dancing over me in celebratory fashion. I can imagine the delight on Your face as I learn and grow, as I'm transformed into Your image. It's the same expression I have when I see a toddler making new discoveries or choosing to obey his parents. You're a proud papa, a daddy who longs to sweep His daughter into His arms for a spin around the dance floor. What a blessed daughter I am too. I'm so happy to bring a smile to Your face. Carry on with the song, Lord—may it spill over into my heart too! Amen.

My Thought Life Matters

Finally, brothers and sisters, whatever is true, whatever is noble, whatever is right, whatever is pure, whatever is lovely, whatever is admirable—if anything is excellent or praiseworthy—think about such things.

PHILIPPIANS 4:8 NIV

When my hope is waning, remind me of this verse, Lord. My thoughts always lead to actions (good or bad), so keep my thoughts on the things that please You. I want to focus on things that are true, not the deceptions of this world or the lies I hear from those who don't know You. I need to focus on noble things—like caring for the poor, tending to those in need. Help me shift my thoughts to doing the right things and remaining pure (a task that isn't always easy in today's society). Lord, may all of my focus be on admirable, lovely things, and may I be a reflection of You to a watching world. Amen.

Peace Is My Guard

*And the peace of God, which transcends
all understanding, will guard your hearts
and your minds in Christ Jesus.*

PHILIPPIANS 4:7 NIV

I'm so fickle, Lord. My emotions go up and down
as life's circumstances present challenges that seem
too much to bear. I'm not proud of this, but when
I'm running on empty (or when my peace is waning)
it's easy to get caught up in the emotions and lose
heart. Thank You for the reminder that Your peace
transcends understanding. I don't have to "get it" to
be peaceful. I can experience peace even when the
storm rages around me. What a revelation, to read
that Your peace serves as a guard around my heart.
Wow! May it shift my focus to You, that I might
live this way, all of my days. Amen.

The Reason for My Hope

But in your hearts revere Christ as Lord. Always be prepared to give an answer to everyone who asks you to give the reason for the hope that you have. But do this with gentleness and respect, keeping a clear conscience, so that those who speak maliciously against your good behavior in Christ may be ashamed of their slander.

1 PETER 3:15—16 NIV

I'm so excited that You are motivated to move on my behalf, Lord. Your Word says I need to be ready to explain the reason for my hope, which tells me that You care a great deal about breathing life into my situations. When people rise up against me, I won't be afraid. I'll be ready to give an answer to naysayers, knowing that You're going to move on my behalf. May others be motivated by this hope inside me. I want to be a good witness for You, Lord. Amen.

I'm Sure of What I Hope For

*"But blessed is the one who trusts in the
Lord, whose confidence is in him."*

JEREMIAH 17:7 NIV

Confident. Sure. These words propel me, Father. I
want to remain confident, even during the rough
seasons. I want to square my shoulders, look my
problems in the eye, and be absolutely convinced
You're going to come through for me. This takes
faith, I know, but You are the Author of faith. So
that's what I ask for today, Lord. Give me faith to
believe for assurance. Give me faith to stand strong
when others around me are falling. May I be sure
of what I hope for, Father. Amen.

Overflowing with Hope

*"He struck the rock so that water gushed out
and streams overflowed. Can he also give
bread or provide meat for his people?"*

PSALM 78:20 ESV

What a day that must have been, Lord, when water
gushed from a rock! I love this picture because it
reminds me that You can make living water out of
even the hardest situation in my life. With one tap
from You, life flows. If the Israelites could trust You
to provide water in the desert, surely I can trust
You to supply my daily needs. My hope is restored
as I see how diligent You care for even the tiniest
details. Thank You for Your provision, Lord, and
this amazing story of hope. I praise You. Amen.

A Shield around Me

Many are saying of me, "God will not deliver him." But you, LORD, are a shield around me, my glory, the One who lifts my head high. I call out to the LORD, and he answers me from his holy mountain. I lie down and sleep; I wake again, because the LORD sustains me. I will not fear though tens of thousands assail me on every side.

PSALM 3:2–6 NIV

I hear what they're saying, Lord. They're pointing fingers and whispering, "She won't make it this time. She's going under." Oh, if only they could see what I'm seeing! You have hemmed me in on every side, giving me refuge, even in the midst of troubles. I'm not afraid when I see the efforts You're putting forth to keep me safe. You're like an impenetrable shield all around me. Let those arrows fling. They won't hit me as long as You're on my side. What hope this brings, Father. What confidence. Today I choose to trust in You. Amen.

A Seed of Hope

Jesus said, "In what way can we show what the holy
nation of God is like? Or what picture-story can
we use to help you understand? It is like a grain of
mustard seed that is planted in the ground. It is the
smallest of all seeds. After it is put in the ground, it
grows and becomes the largest of the spices. It puts
out long branches so birds of the sky can live in it."

MARK 4:30–32 NLV

I love this image of the mustard seed, Father. It's so small, yet it produces one of the largest spices. So many times I feel like my faith is tiny, like that little seed. But You are capable of taking something so small and growing it exponentially. Watching this amazing growth causes hope to grow too. Today I give You my mustard-seed faith. Take it, Lord, and breathe on it, that transformation might take place. Amen.

A Hope That's Wanted

When Jesus saw him lying there and learned that
he had been in this condition for a long time,
he asked him, "Do you want to get well?"

JOHN 5:6 NIV

This is a hard thing to admit, Lord, but sometimes I simply give up hoping. I don't even want to try anymore because I'm afraid I'll be let down. I can relate to the crippled man in today's scripture. He'd been waiting a long time and probably felt his turn would never come. But when Jesus stepped onto the scene, everything changed. I ask You to renew my hope today, Lord. Give me the desire for change. When You ask, "Do you really want this?" I want to be able to answer with a resounding "Yes, Lord!" Only You can bring about the necessary changes in my heart, Father. Today I give You permission to do just that. Amen.

Because There Is Hope

"You will be secure, because there is hope; you will look about you and take your rest in safety."

JOB 11:18 NIV

I love the word *secure*, Lord. This world is anything but! I'm forced to lock my doors day and night. I get nervous sending my kids or grandkids off to school. There's so much to make me anxious. But in You, Father, I place my trust. In You, we all have security beyond anything the world can offer. We don't have to live in fear. Please replace those fears with hope today, Lord. When I put my head on my pillow at night, I want to rest secure in You. Do a work in my heart and mind, I pray. Amen.

Boasting in Our Hope

And we boast in the hope of the glory of God. Not only so, but we also glory in our sufferings, because we know that suffering produces perseverance; perseverance, character; and character, hope. And hope does not put us to shame, because God's love has been poured out into our hearts through the Holy Spirit, who has been given to us.

ROMANS 5:2–5 NIV

Now, this is one time I don't mind boasting, Lord! I love to brag on You. When other people ask me how I keep going, why I don't crater, I tell them the reason for my hope: You. I sing Your praises. It doesn't always make sense to others, but I love sharing how You're growing me into someone different than I used to be. Watching how I persevere is giving others hope, Father. Your hope will never put me to shame. I praise You for the hope You've placed in my heart, Lord. I'm bragging on You today. Amen.

Up from the Grave

Through him you believe in God, who raised him from the dead and glorified him, and so your faith and hope are in God.

1 PETER 1:21 NIV

Hope is a living, breathing thing. I see that now, Lord. I'd always pictured it as a word. A choice. A lifeless thing. But it's not. It's very much alive, quickening my heart even now. Hope boosts the adrenaline. Hope steadies my breathing. Hope shifts my focus. Hope keeps my feet moving. And this hope is alive in me because of the resurrection of Your Son, Jesus. Amazing! When He rose from the dead, He set in motion a hope that refuses to die. What an amazing, motivational gift, Father. Praise You for this hope. Amen.

What I Cannot See

*For in this hope we were saved. Now hope
that is seen is not hope. For who hopes for
what he sees? But if we hope for what we
do not see, we wait for it with patience.*

ROMANS 8:24–25 ESV

This world offers far too many visual images, Lord, and I'm having a hard time filtering them. All I have to do is turn on the news to instantaneously see tragedies happening all over the world. I can watch with my own eyes as hurricanes rip apart towns, as people rise up in anger against one another, as nations are toppled. It's almost too much to take. Instead of fretting over what I can see, please help me to have hope, based on what I can't see. You're in charge. You've got this. Your plans are mighty to save. Today I choose to hope for what I do not see, and I will wait patiently as Your will is done. Amen.

That We Might Have Hope

For whatever was written in former days
was written for our instruction, that through
endurance and through the encouragement
of the Scriptures we might have hope.
ROMANS 15:4 ESV

Sometimes I feel like You're a teacher at the blackboard, Lord, scribbling out reminders of things I've forgotten. (How quickly I walk away from Your Word and forget!) You write the words *endurance* and *instruction* on the board, and I am reminded that this race was never meant to be swift or easy. Then I see words like *encouragement* and *hope*, and I realize You've had the answer to my angst all along. Keep my eyes riveted to Your Word, Lord, that I might have hope. You took the time to make sure those blessed words were written down for my instruction. Thank You for that, Lord. Amen.

A Future Hope

Know also that wisdom is like honey for you: If you find it, there is a future hope for you, and your hope will not be cut off.

PROVERBS 24:14 NIV

Mmm. . .honey. There are so many references to the luscious treat in Your Word, Lord, and I can see why. It adds sweetness to everything it touches. What a revelation, to see that wisdom is like honey. When I approach life's challenges with the wisdom that only You can give, situations are immediately sweetened. And when my situation improves, I'm far more likely to be hopeful about my future. Thank You for the reminder that You've got sweet things in store for me, Father. They're being poured out, even now, like honey for my soul. Now that's a precious promise! I praise You, Lord. Amen.

Heirs according to the Hope

*Because of his grace he made us right
in his sight and gave us confidence
that we will inherit eternal life.*

TITUS 3:7 NLT

Wow, I love the idea of an inheritance, Lord! It's an amazing feeling to know you're so special to someone that they've left you something wonderful. You, Father, have left the most amazing gift of all— eternal life. I won't need to wait for lawyers to dole it out, either. It's available, starting now. It's Your grace that makes this possible. (And trust me, I've needed that grace so many times.) You've somehow made my crooked life straight again. In spite of my mess-ups, You've kept me in the will, Lord. What an amazing Father You are. I praise You. Amen.

Rejoice in Hope

Rejoice in our confident hope. Be patient
in trouble, and keep on praying.

ROMANS 12:12 NLT

Patience. You had to go there, didn't You, Lord? We both know that patience isn't my strong suit! But I'm working on it, Father. When troubles come, I tend to panic, not pray. But today I turn my voice, my woes, my concerns to You. Instead of whining, I choose to praise. I'll rejoice in the fact that You've got this. You're standing right next to me, ready to offer hope. So, instead of running, I'll stand firm. I'll be patient, difficult as that might be. I'll keep on knocking on the doors of heaven and standing firm in the hope You've given me. Thank You, Lord. Amen.

A Sure and Steadfast Anchor

*We have this as a sure and steadfast
anchor of the soul, a hope that enters into
the inner place behind the curtain.*

HEBREWS 6:19 ESV

Strong winds have blown in my life, Lord. Many times, I've wondered if they would toss me overboard. It's comforting to know that You're an anchor in the time of storms. You're sure. You're steadfast. You'll keep me locked in place, standing upright. Because I know I have this anchor, hope stirs in my soul. It's not a false hope, something I drum up in the moment, but a deep, abiding faith that squelches any fears and gives me courage to keep going. Today I choose to cling to You, my immovable, steadfast Father. Thank You for holding all things together. Amen.

I Place My Hope in You

Why are you cast down, O my soul, and why are you in turmoil within me? Hope in God; for I shall again praise him, my salvation and my God.

PSALM 43:5 ESV

Sometimes it's hard to see past the fog. So many dismal things happen in a row and they cloud my vision. But I love the images this verse presents, Lord. When my face is to the ground, when I feel like my heart is twisted in a thousand directions, You long to renew my hope. That's when I need it most, Father! It begins with praise, so I choose to do that today. I won't gaze with fear at the circumstances. Instead, I deliberately choose to lift my eyes toward You, that my hope may be restored. Amen.

My Portion, My Hope

"The LORD is my portion," says my soul,
"therefore I will hope in him."

LAMENTATIONS 3:24 ESV

I know what it's like to be full after a tasty meal, Lord. I've been there plenty of times, especially during the holidays. There's a level of satisfaction when the portion is just right. I've found the same to be true in my relationship with You. You are all I'll ever need. You fill me up on days when I'm feeling empty. You bring hope on days when I'm in crisis. You are truly my all in all, Father. Praise You for that. Amen.

SECTION EIGHT:
"A FUTURE"

*"For I know the plans I have for you," declares
the* LORD, *"plans to prosper you and not to harm
you, plans to give you hope and a future."*

JEREMIAH 29:11 NIV

The road doesn't end here. Think about those words. No matter where you are, no matter what you're facing, God hasn't placed you on a dead end. If He's really a God of hope (and He is), then we've also got to believe that He's got a future planned out for us. What sort of future? That's half of the adventure—finding out! There's no reason to fear what you cannot see when you realize that God has authored the journey. So, what's holding you back? Step into the future He's prepared for you, and do so with joy in your heart.

My Future Is Secure

God saved you by his grace when you believed. And you can't take credit for this; it is a gift from God.

EPHESIANS 2:8 NLT

Every time I fasten my seat belt, I feel secure, Lord. I'm strapped in. Safe. The same is true with my future, now that I've believed in Your Son to save me for all eternity. My spiritual seat belt is fastened tight, but I take absolutely no credit for this. You're holding everything in place. When I come to grips with this truth, I'm assured of something so amazing: I don't have to be scared of tomorrow. I can take bold steps into the unknown. I can see it as an adventure. I'm strapped in tight with You, Father, and You hold the steering wheel. (That fact alone brings the most comfort.) Praise You, Lord. Amen.

Nothing Can Separate Me from Your Love

And I am convinced that nothing can ever separate us from God's love. Neither death nor life, neither angels nor demons, neither our fears for today nor our worries about tomorrow—not even the powers of hell can separate us from God's love. No power in the sky above or in the earth below—indeed, nothing in all creation will ever be able to separate us from the love of God that is revealed in Christ Jesus our Lord.

ROMANS 8:38–39 NLT

I am loved by You today, Lord, and I will be loved tomorrow. Nothing I do, nothing that happens to me, nothing I go through will ever bring an end to Your amazing adoration for me. Because I know Your love will remain, I can trust that it will drive You as Your plans for my life move forward. What peace this brings, Father. Thank You. Amen.

An Enlightened Heart

*I pray that your hearts will be flooded with light
so that you can understand the confident hope
he has given to those he called—his holy people
who are his rich and glorious inheritance.*

EPHESIANS 1:18 NLT

What a lovely image, Lord! I can have an enlightened heart, one flooded with light. Wow. When the light is turned on, my vision is amplified. I'm able to see the future as a positive place, no matter what I'm going through today. And what an awesome reminder that You've prepared an inheritance for me—a rich and glorious one, at that. May the eyes of my heart be completely enlightened so that I never forget You are for me, not against me. Praise You, Father. Amen.

There Will Be a Future

Why, my soul, are you downcast? Why so disturbed
within me? Put your hope in God, for I will
yet praise him, my Savior and my God.

PSALM 42:5 NIV

There's a sense of foreboding that hits me sometimes, Father. I feel like my hopes are dashed.
There's no future for me. I confess, I often feel like
You've overlooked me and are more focused on
others. Thank You for the assurance in Your Word
that there will be a future for me. I understand my
role, Lord: I'm to see wisdom in my soul (my heart
and mind). Though this isn't always easy, I will give
it my best shot and trust You with the rest. Amen.

Every Step of the Way

The temptations in your life are no different from what others experience. And God is faithful. He will not allow the temptation to be more than you can stand. When you are tempted, he will show you a way out so that you can endure.

1 CORINTHIANS 10:13 NLT

Lord, I take comfort in the fact that You've made a way of escape for me, even in my darkest hour. If it's true that You have plans for my future, then I have to believe You have a way to escape today's tragedy in order to take me there. No matter how difficult the road ahead, Father, I trust that You will lead me every step of the way. Amen.

Surely There Is a Future

Surely there is a future, and your hope will not be cut off.

PROVERBS 23:18 ESV

I love the word *surely*, Lord. For surely there is a future. It's solid. It's set in stone. It's immovable. I can't see it yet, but that's where the adventure begins. My inability to see means that I have no choice but to "let go and let God," as the old saying goes. So that's what I choose today. And I do so, Father, with the assurance that surely there is a future for me, one You've already got mapped out to a T. What hope this brings, what joy! Thank You, Lord, for the "surelys" in my life. Amen.

You Establish My Steps

The heart of man plans his way, but
the Lord establishes his steps.

PROVERBS 16:9 ESV

Father, my very steps are ordered. I can't see the footprints that You've laid out for me, but You can, and even at this very moment, You're guiding me to walk paths set before me. If I get off course, Lord, lead me back. I want to walk confidently into the future, knowing that my direction is set and my course sure. How deep and abiding my trust in You is as I think that through. Amen.

What Tomorrow Brings

Come now, you who say, "Today or tomorrow we will go into such and such a town and spend a year there and trade and make a profit"—yet you do not know what tomorrow will bring. What is your life? For you are a mist that appears for a little time and then vanishes. Instead you ought to say, "If the Lord wills, we will live and do this or that."

JAMES 4:13–15 ESV

I'm such a planner, Lord. I know You know this. You see my lists. You know the motivations of my heart. Truth is, I don't know what tomorrow will bring. I can plan all I like, but my future is wholly in Your hands. Today I submit myself to Your will—not just for today but all the days to come. Remind me daily that You are in control, not me. And may I never forget that Your idea of a bright tomorrow is far greater than my own. I can trust You, Lord. Amen.

Greater Than My Heart

*This is how we know that we belong to the truth
and how we set our hearts at rest in his presence:
If our hearts condemn us, we know that God is
greater than our hearts, and he knows everything.*

1 JOHN 3:19–20 NIV

Sometimes I'm racked with guilt, Lord. I'm not talking about conviction—I'm talking about full-out can't-sleep, can't-eat, can't-think guilt. I have such a hard time taking steps forward because my feet are stuck in the muck and mire of what I've done. Thank You for the promise that You can (and do) set my heart at rest. You are greater than my heart. What a relief! My heart is heavy, burdened. Today I give it (and this guilt) to You, Father. Forgive me for the wrongs I've done, and ease the weight so that I can begin to move into a bright future with You. Amen.

Mysteries Revealed

*"He reveals the deep things of darkness
and brings utter darkness into the light."*

JOB 12:22 NIV

I love a good mystery, Lord, but not always when I'm the one who's mystified or confused. When it comes to my life and my future, I want to see where I'm headed. But my life is like a great novel, isn't it, Father? There are whodunits all over the place! And only You know where the story will take me next. I will do my best to calm my heart as Your great mysteries are revealed, step by step. I'll try not to panic when the twists and turns are darkened by night skies. I'll keep my focus on You, Lord. I know You will never fail me. You have revelations aplenty coming my way. What an adventure! Amen.

My Inheritance

*Praise be to the God and Father of our Lord
Jesus Christ! In his great mercy he has given
us new birth into a living hope through the
resurrection of Jesus Christ from the dead, and
into an inheritance that can never perish, spoil or
fade. This inheritance is kept in heaven for you.*

1 PETER 1:3—4 NIV

I'm beginning to understand what it feels like,
Father, to have an inheritance, one that truly matters.
Through Your Son, You've given me the hope, the
assurance of heaven. Wow, what a gift! Any worldly
inheritance would eventually run out, but the one
You have in store for me will last forever. No rust
will corrode it. No moths will consume it. No thief
can steal it. My inheritance is secure in You, Father.
What joy to have such a loving Father. Amen.

Passport in Heaven

But our citizenship is in heaven. And we eagerly await a Savior from there, the Lord Jesus Christ.

PHILIPPIANS 3:20 NIV

Traveling is so much fun, Lord. I love the journeys I've taken in my life—whether by car, boat, or plane. Getting to my destination is half the fun! The same is true in my journey with You, Father. You're leading me toward the most beautiful destination of all: heaven. Oh, how I'm enjoying the journey, and I feel sure (based on what I've read in Your Word) that the destination will be beyond my wildest dreams. I can almost picture it now. Best of all, my passport is ready. Thanks to Your work on the cross, Jesus, my journey has already begun. Praise You for giving me a heavenly passport, Lord. Amen.

New Compassions Every Day

Because of the LORD's great love we are not consumed, for his compassions never fail. They are new every morning; great is your faithfulness.
LAMENTATIONS 3:22—23 NIV

I get it, Lord. I get why You don't want me to go to bed angry. You don't want to let the woes of one day spill over into the next. When I fall asleep in a peaceful state, I can awake to new beginnings. In the same way, I'm grateful that You don't go to bed angry with me when I've had a less than stellar day. You love me, forgive me, give me a pat on the back, and promise that Your compassions will be new tomorrow morning. What a faithful God You are. Left to my own devices, I would get stuck in the angst of today. But with You, my future is secure, because Your compassions never fail. Thank You, Lord! Amen.

Wide Vision

For he views the ends of the earth and
sees everything under the heavens.

JOB 28:24 NIV

It's such a relief to know that Your vision is wide, Father. You can see from one end of the universe to the other, from every star to every planet to the next breath I'm going to take. You see it all and orchestrate it with Your majestic hand. Because I know Your vision is remarkable, I can count on You to lead and guide. If You can see what's hiding beyond the farthest star, surely You can see what the future holds for me, Your child. Praise You, Lord! Amen.

The Weight of Glory

For our present troubles are small and won't last
very long. Yet they produce for us a glory that
vastly outweighs them and will last forever!
So we don't look at the troubles we can see now;
rather, we fix our gaze on things that cannot be
seen. For the things we see now will soon be gone,
but the things we cannot see will last forever.

2 CORINTHIANS 4:17—18 NLT

Oh, how the weight of my troubles can drag me down, Father. Sometimes I feel like I'm down on my knees, crawling along. But I'm grateful today for a different kind of weight—the weight of Your glory. You're developing me, Lord, and forming me into Your image. Thank You for fixing my eyes on the things I cannot see so that I can freely walk toward You. Amen.

You Go before Me

"Do not be afraid or discouraged, for the LORD will personally go ahead of you. He will be with you; he will neither fail you nor abandon you."

DEUTERONOMY 31:8 NLT

How secure I felt as a child, Lord, when my mother or father would hold my hand and lead me alongside them. Their long, confident strides gave me courage to trust in where we were headed. The same is true with You. Your strides are long and confident and often stretch far beyond mine, but with Your hand in mine, I feel as secure as I did all those years ago. I'm completely confident that You won't take off running and leave me in the dust. Even when You step out in front of me, You stick close. You care far too much about me to leave me on my own. What a wonderful Father You are! Amen.

Free Indeed

"So if the Son sets you free, you are truly free."

JOHN 8:36 NLT

I love the word *truly*, Lord. When You set me free from my past, my addictions, my failures, my woes, my bad attitudes, my habits, my poor relationships, You *truly* set me free. Indeed. How foolish would I be to turn back now, when You've broken chains that held me bound and released me to new life in You? Oh, Father, You've brought me so far. I don't even like to look back to the way things used to be, except to learn from my mistakes. You've got such an amazing future planned out for me. I wouldn't want to miss a thing. So I'll stand on the outside of those prison walls, forever grateful You were willing to rescue me, Lord. Truly! Amen.

Oh, Wise One

Get all the advice and instruction you can,
so you will be wise the rest of your life.

PROVERBS 19:20 NLT

Sometimes I feel like a little sponge, Lord. I sit there on the counter, dry as a bone, wondering why my life isn't productive. Then I remember why things are going so poorly. I've ceased to spend time with You and in Your Word. So, I race back to Your arms, ready to admit just how much I need You. You brush away every tear and whisper words of great caring into my ears. Only when I spend adequate time with You will I acquire the necessary wisdom to get through the narrow channels in my life, Lord. So today I choose to remain close. May I be like that little sponge, soaking up all the wisdom I can, both today and in all the days to come. Amen.

Broken Chains

Then they cried to the LORD in their trouble, and he saved them from their distress. He brought them out of darkness, the utter darkness, and broke away their chains. Let them give thanks to the LORD for his unfailing love and his wonderful deeds for mankind, for he breaks down gates of bronze and cuts through bars of iron.

PSALM 107:13–16 NIV

Wow, what a picture of Your power, Lord! You've broken through gates of bronze and bars of iron to get to me. Even when I was in my deepest, darkest place, You came barreling through, ready to release my chains. And all so that I could have a future. You didn't want to see me bound up, Father, living below my potential. That's the kind of unfailing love You had for me then and have for me even now. You've always wanted to lift me to higher places. Praise You for Your great, inspiring passion for Your children. Amen.

Your Good Pleasure

*"Do not be afraid, little flock, for your Father
has been pleased to give you the kingdom."*

LUKE 12:32 NIV

The kingdom. Oh, how I love speaking that word.
Kingdom. Sometimes I feel like a princess in a castle
tower, surveying all of the lands below that belong
to her father, the king. You are the great and mighty
King, Lord, and I'm in awe of Your kingdom—
both the earthly kingdom and the heavenly kingdom to come. What truly awes me is that You've
chosen to give all of this: the pleasures of a relationship with You here on earth and a heavenly
home besides. You must really care a lot about
me, Lord. I am Your humble daughter, completely
wowed by her Daddy God. Amen.

SECTION NINE:
WRAPPING IT UP

"For I know the plans I have for you," declares
the LORD, "plans to prosper you and not to harm
you, plans to give you hope and a future."
JEREMIAH 29:11 NIV

We've learned so much about the heart of God as we've looked at Jeremiah 29:11. He knows all. He's got great plans for His kids, plans that are beautifully tailored to us as individuals. He longs to prosper us—in all areas of life. We can trust that He's out to do us good, not harm, to give us a hope and a future. When we think on all these things, we begin to see our lives as a marvelous race, one designed just for us. Praise the Lord! He's going before us even now to prepare a way that leads from this very moment, all the way to eternity.

Wherever We Go

"Be strong and courageous. Do not be afraid or terrified because of them, for the LORD your God goes with you; he will never leave you nor forsake you."

DEUTERONOMY 31:6 NIV

I'm remembering my childhood, Lord—how I would climb into the backseat of the car and let my parents take me from place to place. I didn't always know where we were headed, but from the moment I got in that car, I knew I would be safe. The same is true with You, Father. Wherever I go, whether it's to a local supermarket or a mission field halfway across the globe, You're behind the wheel, carrying me safely to where I need to be. What a comfort, to trust in the One who created me to lead me safely on. Amen.

Your Great Love

*For God so loved the world that he gave his
one and only Son, that whoever believes in
him shall not perish but have eternal life.*

JOHN 3:16 NIV

It's the ultimate verse, Lord, the one we hang all
of our hopes and dreams on. Your love—that vast,
immeasurable, transforming love—offers us new
hope. Your plan for us always included a happily-
ever-after with You. What an amazing romancer
You are! You woo us to You then provide life eternal.
But what a sacrifice You made, sending Your Son
so that all of this would be possible. There are no
words to express my gratitude, but I will try, Lord.
With all of my life, my actions, my thoughts, my
motivations, I will try. Amen.

I Live by Faith

I have been crucified with Christ and I no longer live, but Christ lives in me. The life I now live in the body, I live by faith in the Son of God, who loved me and gave himself for me.

GALATIANS 2:20 NIV

It's not about me anymore, Lord. It's all about You. Oh, I know—it used to be about me. Always. My way or the highway. But those days are gone. The old me has vanished. In her place: Jesus Christ, Your Son! This new outlook has taken some getting used to. (I was, after all, looking out for me, myself, and I for a very long time.) But, after all You've done for me, how could I desire any other path? I choose to live by faith in the One who gave Himself for me. May every attitude be a reflection of that decision, Father. Amen.

To the End of the Age

"And surely I am with you always,
to the very end of the age."

MATTHEW 28:20 NIV

It's probably a good thing that I don't know how long I'll live, Lord. I don't know the number of my days, but You do. I'm not counting down the minutes, but I am doing my best to live each day with purpose, ready to see Your plans fulfilled in my life. Best of all, I'm enjoying getting to know You more with each passing day. No matter how many years I have left, every one will be spent with Your hand in mine. How remarkable to know that the Creator of the universe cares enough about me to walk with me, every day of my life. Praise You for that, Lord. Amen.

Until It Is Finally Finished

And I am certain that God, who began the good work within you, will continue his work until it is finally finished on the day when Christ Jesus returns.

PHILIPPIANS 1:6 NLT

You're a "never give up" kind of God, and I love that about You. When You start things, You finish them. I wish I could say I had that attribute, but many times I begin projects and give up halfway through. I throw in the towel often before I've even given things a chance. You won't give up on me, Lord, even when I feel like giving up on myself. Whew. That's a comfort. Your work will continue all the way to completion. I don't know what the "completed" me will look like, but You do—and You've already begun the work to get me there. Thanks for hanging in there! Amen.

A Face-to-Face Meeting

When I awake, I will see you
face to face and be satisfied.
PSALM 17:15 NLT

So many of the situations in my life are muddy, Lord. Unclear. Blurry. Sometimes I wish I had a magic mirror like the ones in fairy tales so that I could clearly see what's coming. Thank goodness that You know. And though my vision is imperfect, there's coming a day when everything will make perfect sense. I will see You face-to-face and receive all of the answers to the lingering questions in my life. Until that day, I choose to trust in Your plans, Father, even when they look a bit fuzzy around the edges. Amen.

Right Paths

He renews my strength. He guides me along
right paths, bringing honor to his name.

PSALM 23:3 NLT

Choices, choices. They're everywhere! I could turn to the right. Or the left. I could go forward. Or backward. I could take this job. Or that job. Or even that other job. I could date this person. Or that person. Or the other person. With so many paths in front of me (and so many voices urging me to go this way or that), I could find myself headed in the wrong direction in a hurry. Today I commit myself to listen carefully to Your voice alone so that I can take the right road. And as I step out onto it, I will receive strength for the journey that only You can give. With every step, I will do my best to bring honor and glory to Your name. Amen.

Victory!

But thank God! He gives us victory over sin and death through our Lord Jesus Christ. So, my dear brothers and sisters, be strong and immovable. Always work enthusiastically for the Lord, for you know that nothing you do for the Lord is ever useless.

1 CORINTHIANS 15:57—58 NLT

I love a good victory, Father, whether it's at a ball game, during a volatile political season, or in an argument with an adversary. But there's a greater victory than the ones I see in the temporal realm. When You died on the cross, Jesus, the ultimate victory over sin and death was won. This victory leads to eternal life for all who call on Your name. How can I ever thank You enough for winning that battle on my behalf, Lord? I commit myself enthusiastically to share the good news of what You've done so that others can share in this victory too. Amen.

Understanding Your Will

Show me the right path, O LORD;
point out the road for me to follow.

PSALM 25:4 NLT

So often I rail against what I do not understand. It's hard to move forward when what's in front of me makes no sense at all. But You're teaching me, Father, that one thing is a given: You have my best interest at heart. So, I choose to keep moving, even when I'm perplexed by the twists and turns in the road. I don't want to be thoughtless. I want every step in my journey to be carefully thought out so that I know without a doubt what You're wanting me to do. If I begin to veer in the wrong direction, please take hold of my hand and lead me back to the right road. May I listen carefully so that I can understand, Lord. Thank You for Your guidance! Amen.

You See My Steps

"His eyes are on the ways of mortals;
he sees their every step."

JOB 34:21 NIV

Remember that time, Lord, when I missed a step and fell? As I careened downward, I felt the pain of impact. Oh, how it hurt; how I wished I'd seen that stair step in advance to better navigate my way. You healed my broken body, but You also taught me a life lesson. All of my steps are visible to You. Even in the darkest night as I feel my way along, You see clearly. Move me with confidence toward the future You have planned for me, Father. Even when I can't see where I'm headed, I know that You do. Every step I take is visible, even the bumbling ones. I give You my feet. Be my compass. Be my guide. I will follow where You lead. Amen.

Living and Active

For the word of God is alive and active. Sharper than any double-edged sword, it penetrates even to dividing soul and spirit, joints and marrow; it judges the thoughts and attitudes of the heart.

HEBREWS 4:12 NIV

When I open my Bible, Lord, it's almost like the words jump out at me. I can see them as a mighty sword, piercing my heart and cutting to the very place where I need them most. It's an amazing thing, Father, to see how You match the verses with the situations I'm walking through. On those days when I'm feeling a little lost, when I'm not sure where the road is taking me, out springs a verse, giving clear direction. Your Word is alive, Lord! It's breathing. It's active. It's relatable, even in the twenty-first century. How can I ever thank You enough for speaking life to Your children? Praise You for Your Word. Amen.

Knowing and Known

*"I am the good shepherd; I know
my sheep and my sheep know me."*

JOHN 10:14 NIV

You've placed so many wonderful people in my life, Lord. I've come to know so many. I've discovered, though, that to be known requires a more intimate relationship. That's what You're asking of me as Your plans are laid out before me: to know and be known. May I know You more as I delve into a deeper relationship with You. As Your plans for my life unfold (and what fun, to discover these plans day by day), I feel like I'm getting to know You even more. I'm also getting to know myself, which has been great fun—though a little frightening at times, since I'm so far from perfect. Oh, to know and be known by my Creator! Oh, to walk in intimate relationship with others. What a privilege. Thank You, Father. Amen.

A Strong Support

"For the eyes of the LORD range throughout the earth to strengthen those whose hearts are fully committed to him."

2 CHRONICLES 16:9 NIV

It's fascinating to think about Your eyesight, Lord. How is it possible to see all of the universe—every planet, every continent, every country, every city, every neighborhood, every home—all at once? I marvel at the very idea. It brings a smile to my face when I think about the fact that You are watching those of us who've committed our lives to You, so that You can bring strength. Please look on me today, Father. Give me the strength I need to travel down this road You've placed me on. Thanks for keeping such a good eye on me, Lord. Amen.

Wisdom and Might

"To God belong wisdom and power;
counsel and understanding are his."

JOB 12:13 NIV

I am created in Your image, Father, and I'm so grateful. I know that wisdom and power are Yours, but I also know that as Your child, I can be wise and powerful too. (One of the perks of being Your child!) Your counsel is the best. I know, because I've applied it to my life on so many occasions. But I'm glad You're teaching me to counsel others, as well. May Your understanding and Your wisdom be mine as I walk this road You've laid before me. Have I mentioned how grateful I am that I'm Your daughter, Lord? Amen.

Carving Channels

"He cuts out channels in the rocks,
and his eye sees every precious thing."

JOB 28:10 NKJV

Father, what a revelation to know that You go ahead of me and actually carve out channels through the rocks. I would be like a miner lost in the darkened hollows of the shaft if not for You! How remarkable, to think that Your eye sees even the most beautiful gems in the rock You're carving out. Are there diamonds along my path, Father? If so, give me Your vision to see as the road ahead is carved. What a beautiful story You're writing, Lord! I'm so honored You would go to such trouble for me. Amen.

Broken in the Depths

By wisdom the LORD laid the earth's foundations,
by understanding he set the heavens in place;
by his knowledge the watery depths were
divided, and the clouds let drop the dew.

PROVERBS 3:19—20 NIV

What an amazing scripture, Lord! By Your knowledge, the oceans, lakes, rivers, streams, and ponds were broken up. Each became its own entity. I know from personal experience that the breaking process isn't always easy, but the outcome is always worth it. Today I give You permission, as You lay forth the plans for my life, to break me in the depths. Break my heart for what breaks Yours. Break my will, so that my selfish desires will fade. Break my pride, that I may be more like You. May I, in the brokenness, become more like You, my Creator. Amen.

You Are the Potter

Woe to those who go to great depths to hide their plans from the LORD, who do their work in darkness and think, "Who sees us? Who will know?" You turn things upside down, as if the potter were thought to be like the clay! Shall what is formed say to the one who formed it, "You did not make me"? Can the pot say to the potter, "You know nothing"?

ISAIAH 29:15–16 NIV

You are my Potter, Father. You've placed me on the wheel, a formless lump of clay. With Your hands firmly guiding the process, You've shaped me into a visionary, one who sees the vast possibilities for my life. I love what I'm seeing. As You morph me from season to season, I'm growing—spiritually, emotionally, and psychologically. I give You full permission to continue Your work, that Your plan for my life might be all You intended. Thank You, my Potter! Amen.

You Stretched Out the Heavens

"He made the earth by his power; he founded the world by his wisdom and stretched out the heavens by his understanding."

JEREMIAH 51:15 NIV

I can almost picture it now, Lord. Your mighty hand, grabbing hold over the corners of heaven and tugging them into place. You stretched, and things were established. The same has been true in my life, Lord. Your plans have stretched me beyond what I thought I was capable of. Your wisdom has grown me into someone who trusts You more, walks on water with greater assurance, and looks toward the future as a hopeful place. How can I ever thank You enough for growing me into a stronger woman of God? My heart is Yours, Lord. Amen.

Called Forth

"Who has done this and carried it through,
calling forth the generations from the
beginning? I, the LORD—with the first of
them and with the last—I am he."

ISAIAH 41:4 NIV

There's a calling on my life, Lord. I sense it. I feel it. I appreciate it. I choose to respond to it. You've called me with a unique and personalized calling, one that fits like a satin glove. I hear what You're whispering in my ear, that Your intense love for me propelled You to stir my heart to action. Thank You, Father. Knowing that the King of the universe has taken the time to plot, strategize, and implement a plan for my life is amazing. What a blessing! Amen.

Perfect in Knowledge

"Do you know how the clouds hang poised,
those wonders of him who has perfect knowledge?"

JOB 37:16 NIV

Lord, I remember so clearly the times I had to take tests in school, how I prayed for Your divine intervention. I wanted everything I'd learned to root itself in my heart so that I could have a ready answer for every question. How marvelous to realize that You are perfect in knowledge. There's not a test question out there that You can't answer. My mind can't fathom Your ability, Father, but I marvel in the fact that Your ways are perfect. With that in mind, I choose to trust You as I move forward with Your hand in mine. Amen.

More Inspiration for Your Beautiful Soul

God Calls You Worthy
978-1-64352-474-0

God Calls You Forgiven
978-1-64352-637-9

God Calls You Beautiful
978-1-64352-710-9

God Calls You Loved
978-1-64352-804-5

God Calls You Chosen
978-1-64352-926-4

These delightful devotionals—created just
for you—will encourage and inspire your soul
with deeply rooted truths from God's Word

Flexible Casebound / $12.99 each